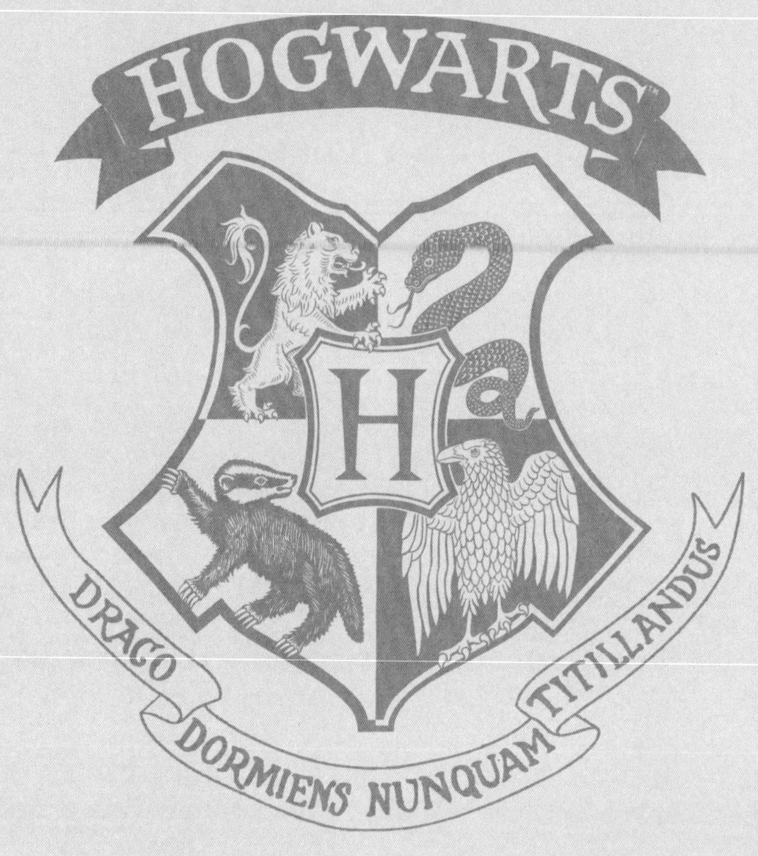

PROPERTY OF:

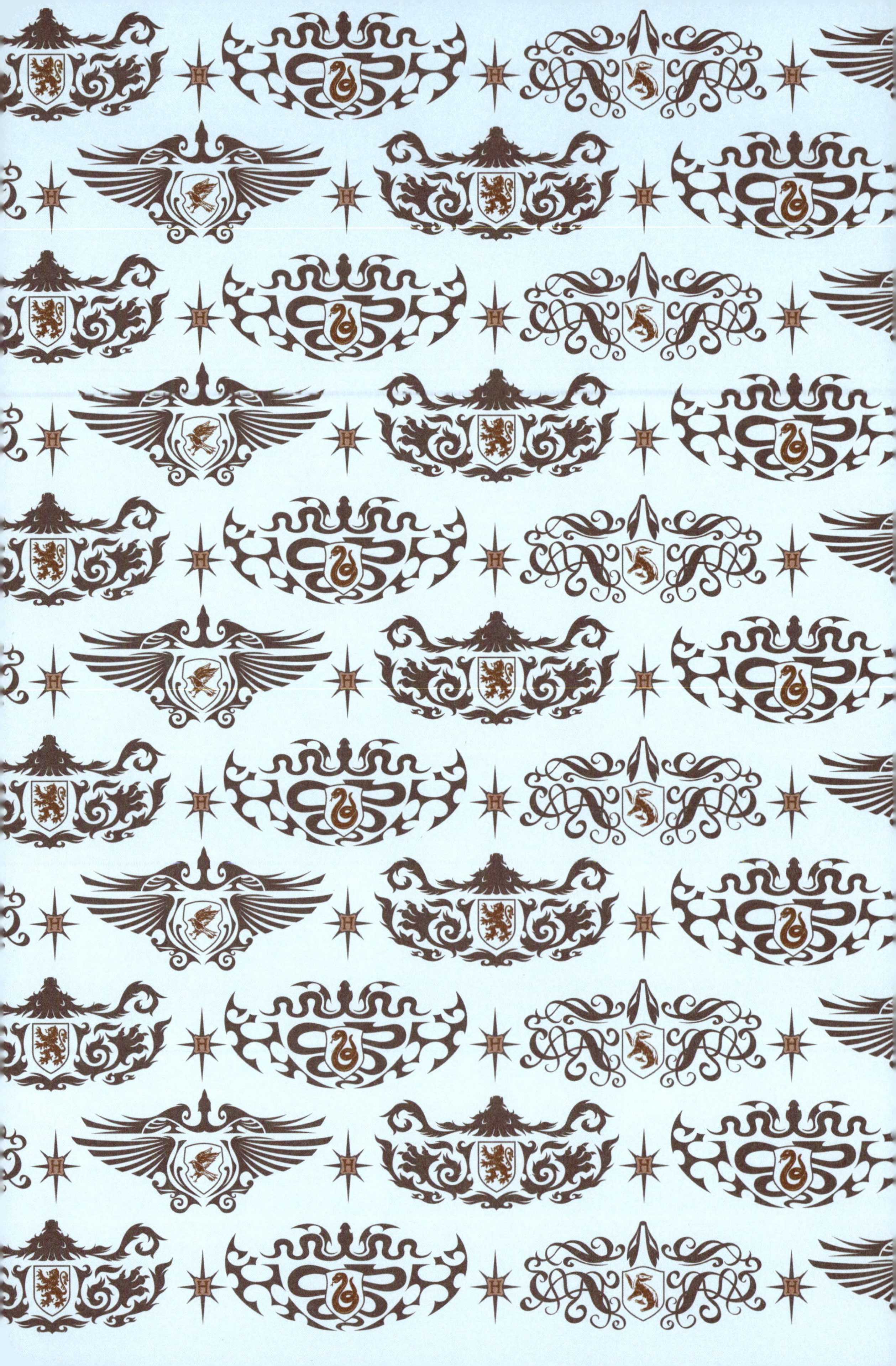

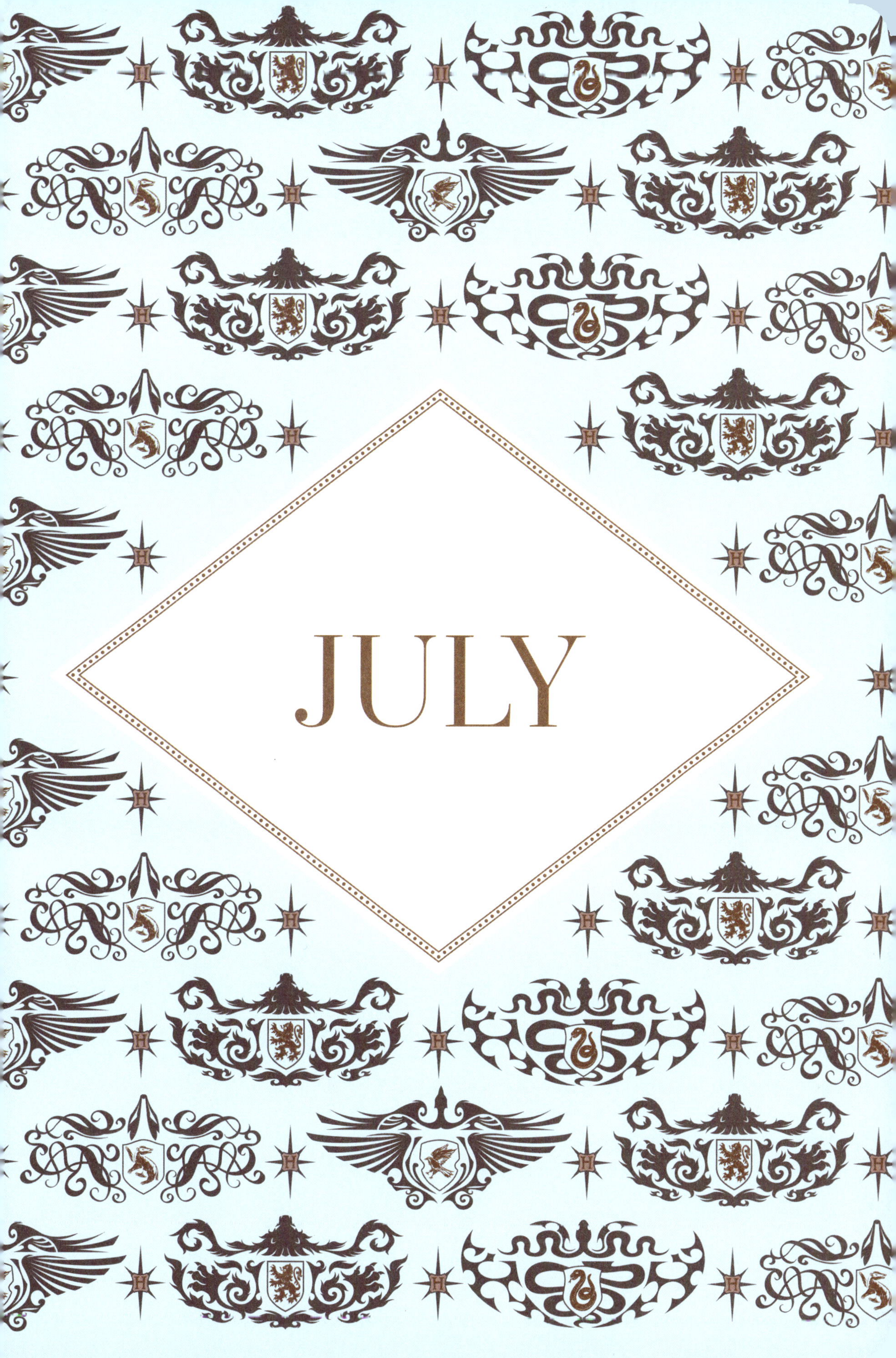

JULY

JULY 2023

SUNDAY	MONDAY	TUESDAY	WEDNESDAY
2	3	4 Independence Day	5
9	10	11	12
16	17	18	19
23	24	25	26
30	31 Harry Potter's Birthday		

THURSDAY	FRIDAY	SATURDAY	Notes
		1	
6	7	8	
13	14	15	
20	21	22	
27	28	29	

JUNE 26–JULY 2

26 Monday

27 Tuesday

28 Wednesday

NOTES

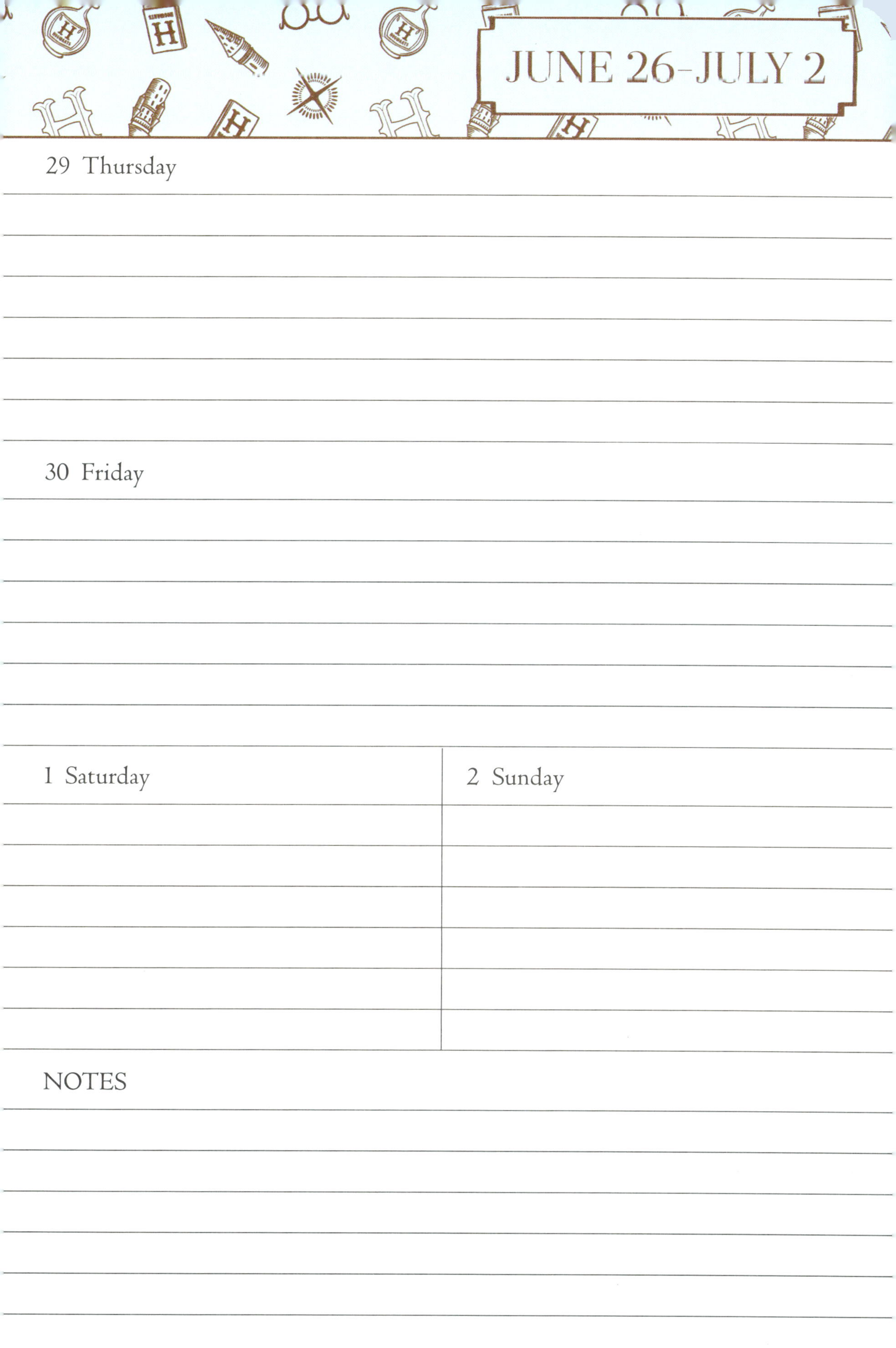

29 Thursday

30 Friday

1 Saturday

2 Sunday

NOTES

3 Monday

4 Tuesday   INDEPENDENCE DAY

5 Wednesday

NOTES

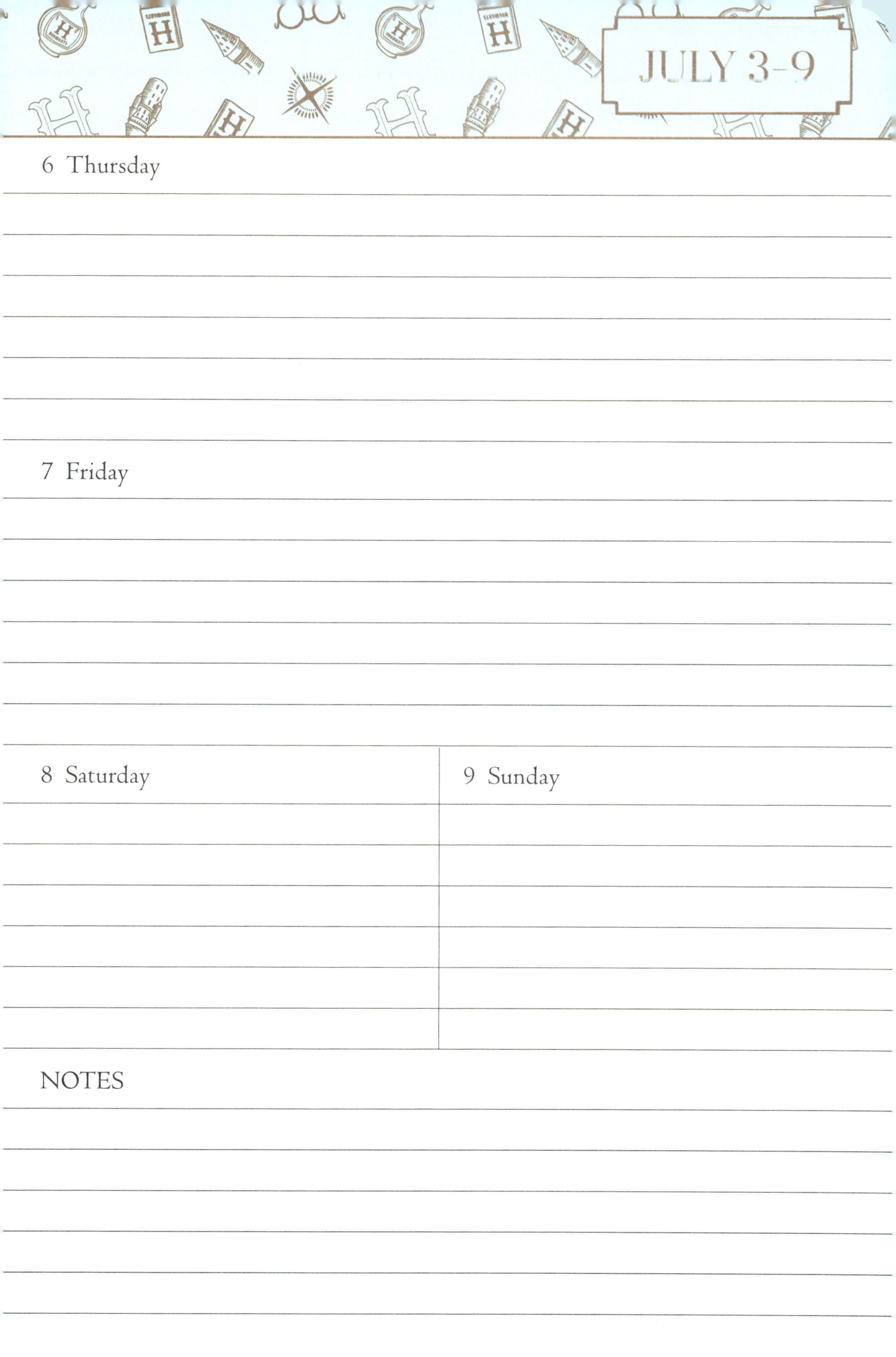

6 Thursday

7 Friday

8 Saturday

9 Sunday

NOTES

JULY 10-16

10 Monday

11 Tuesday

12 Wednesday

NOTES

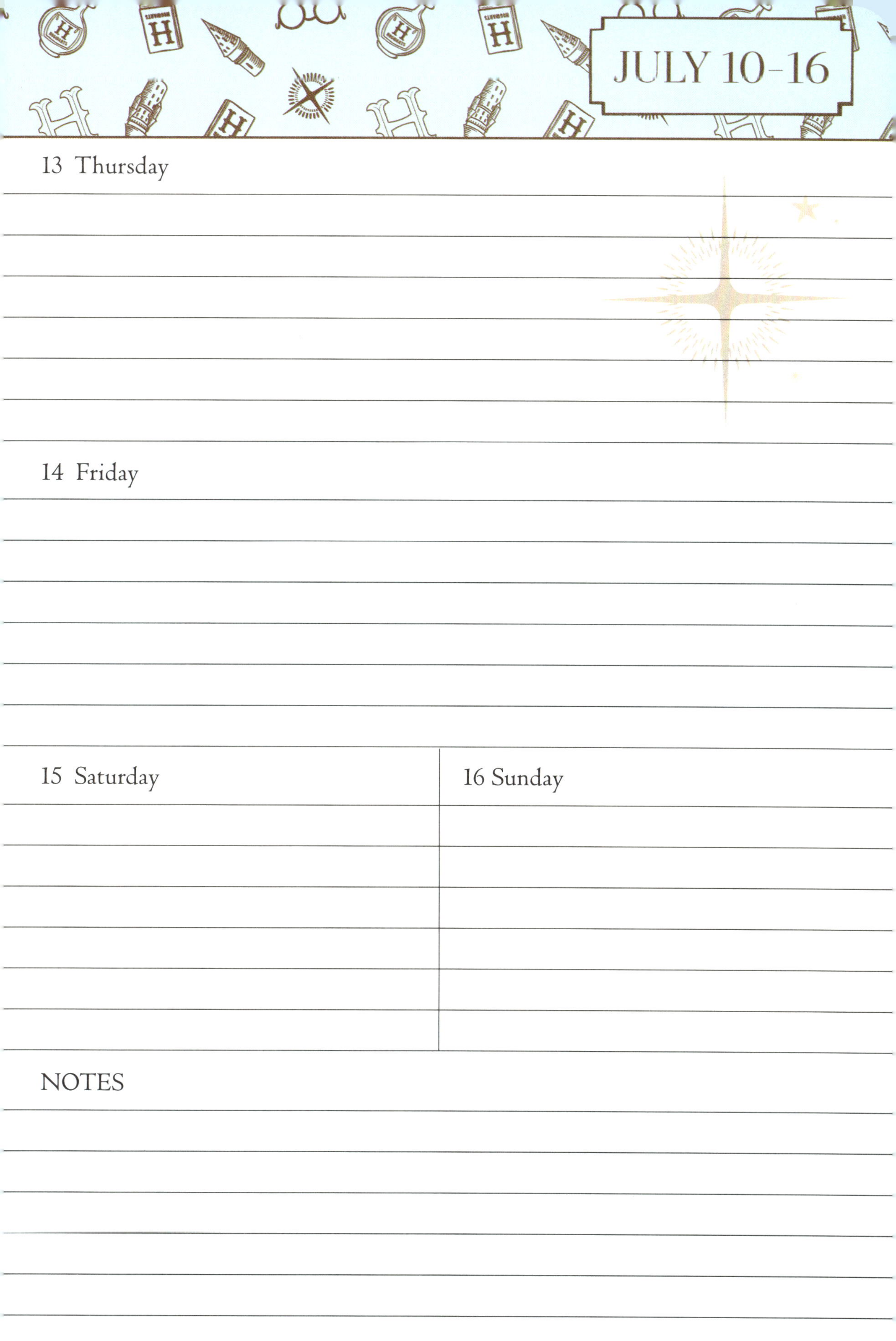

13 Thursday

14 Friday

15 Saturday

16 Sunday

NOTES

17 Monday

18 Tuesday

19 Wednesday

NOTES

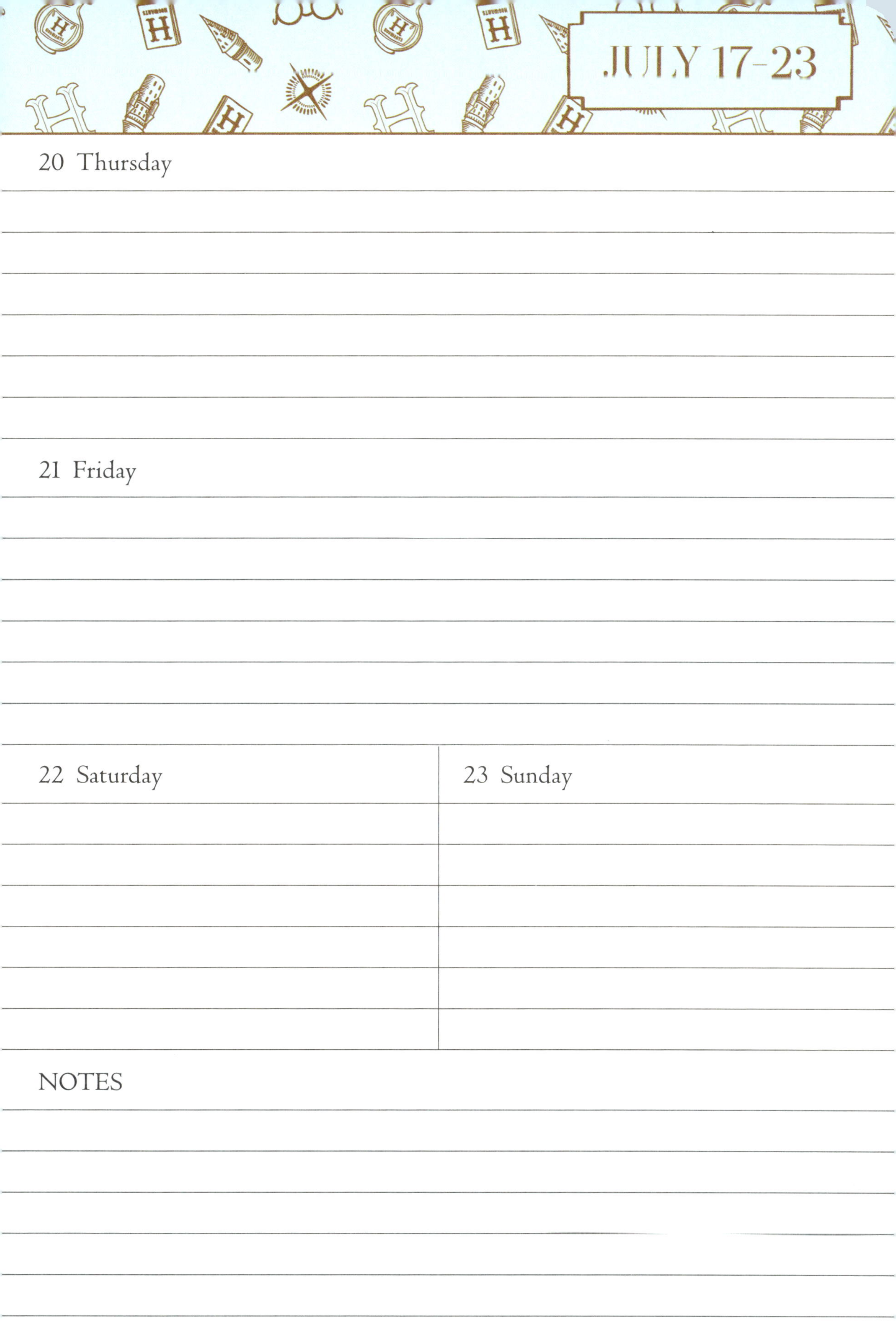

20 Thursday

21 Friday

22 Saturday

23 Sunday

NOTES

JULY 24-30

24 Monday

25 Tuesday

26 Wednesday

NOTES

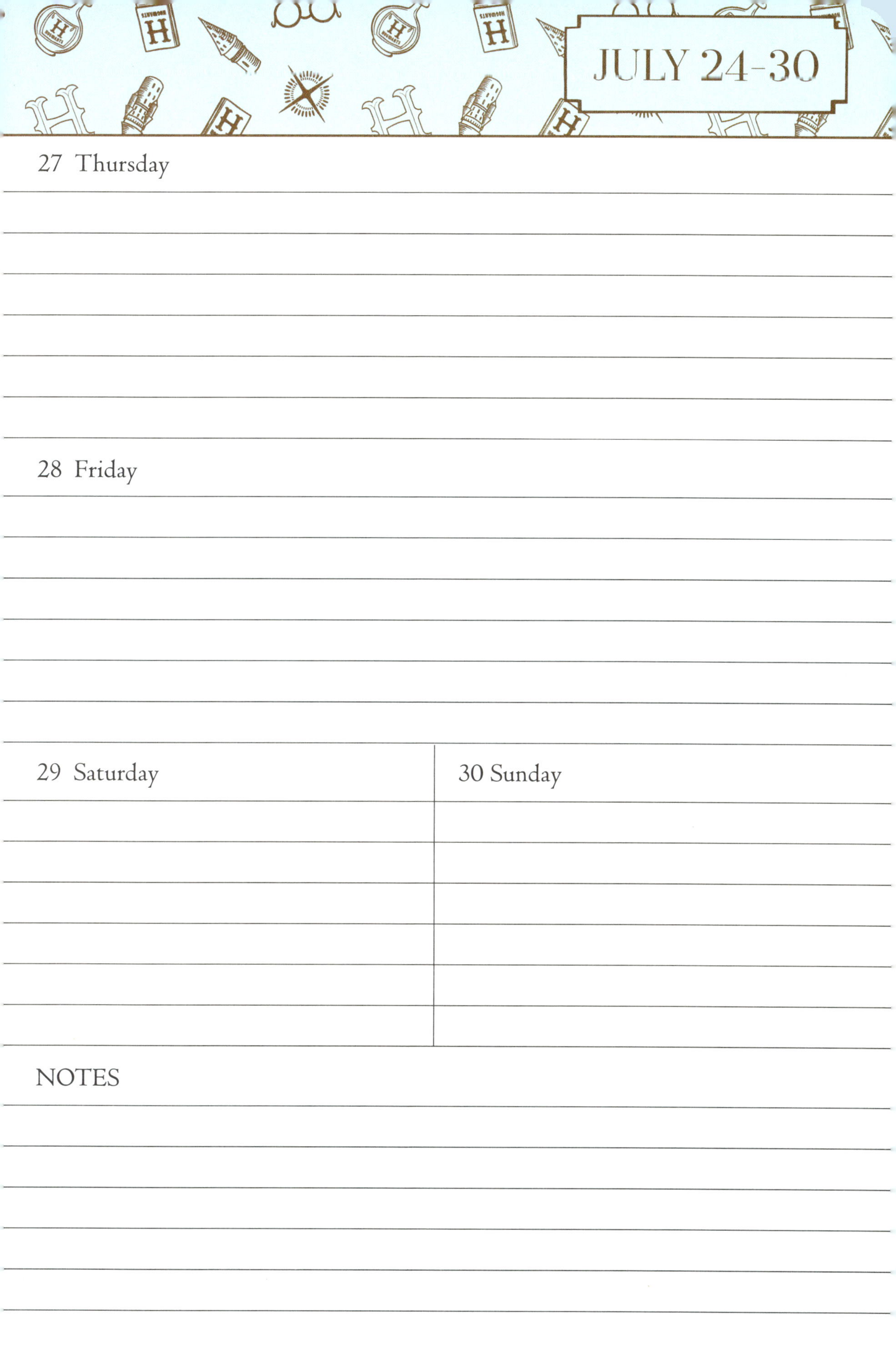

27 Thursday

28 Friday

29 Saturday

30 Sunday

NOTES

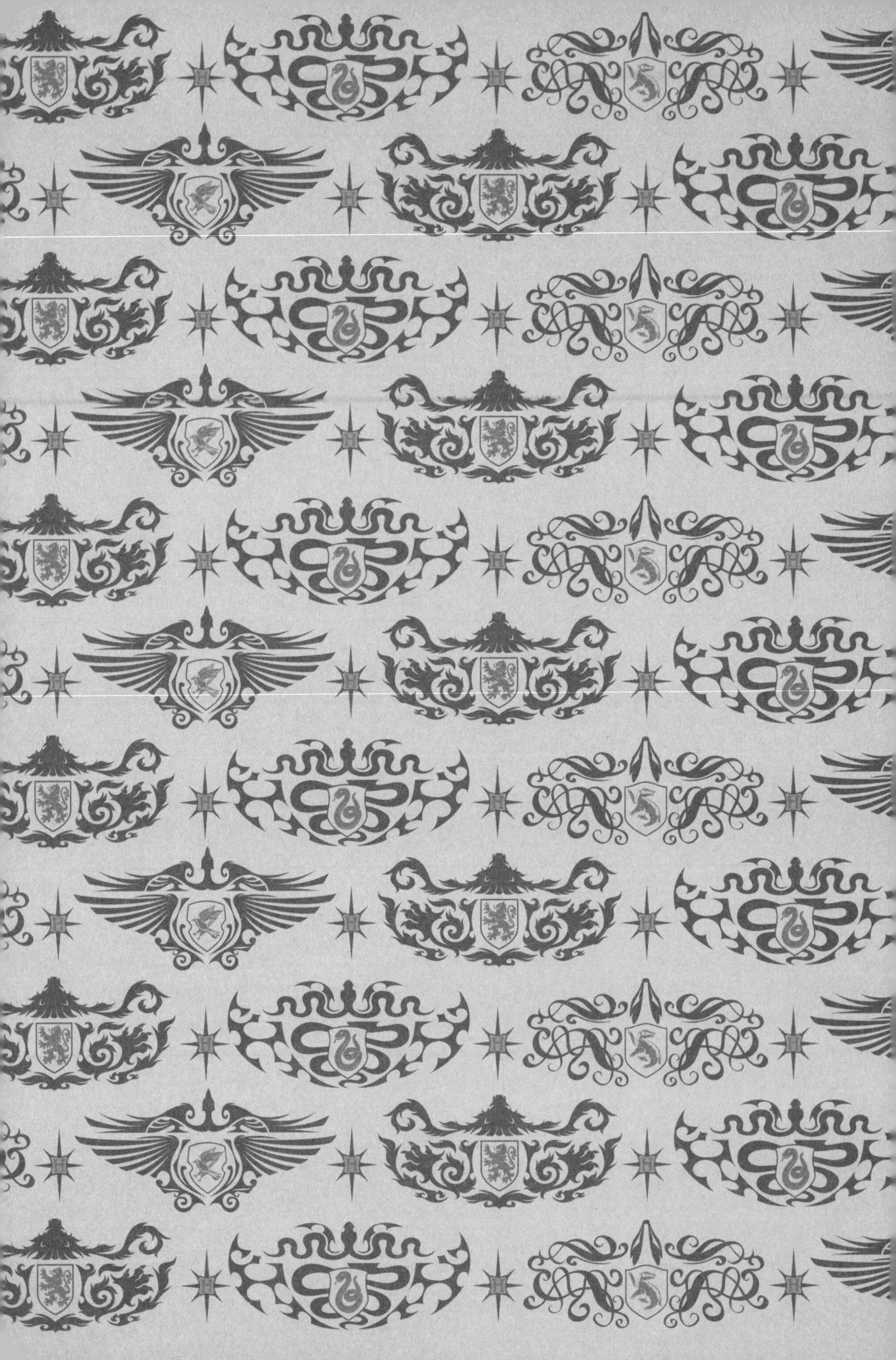

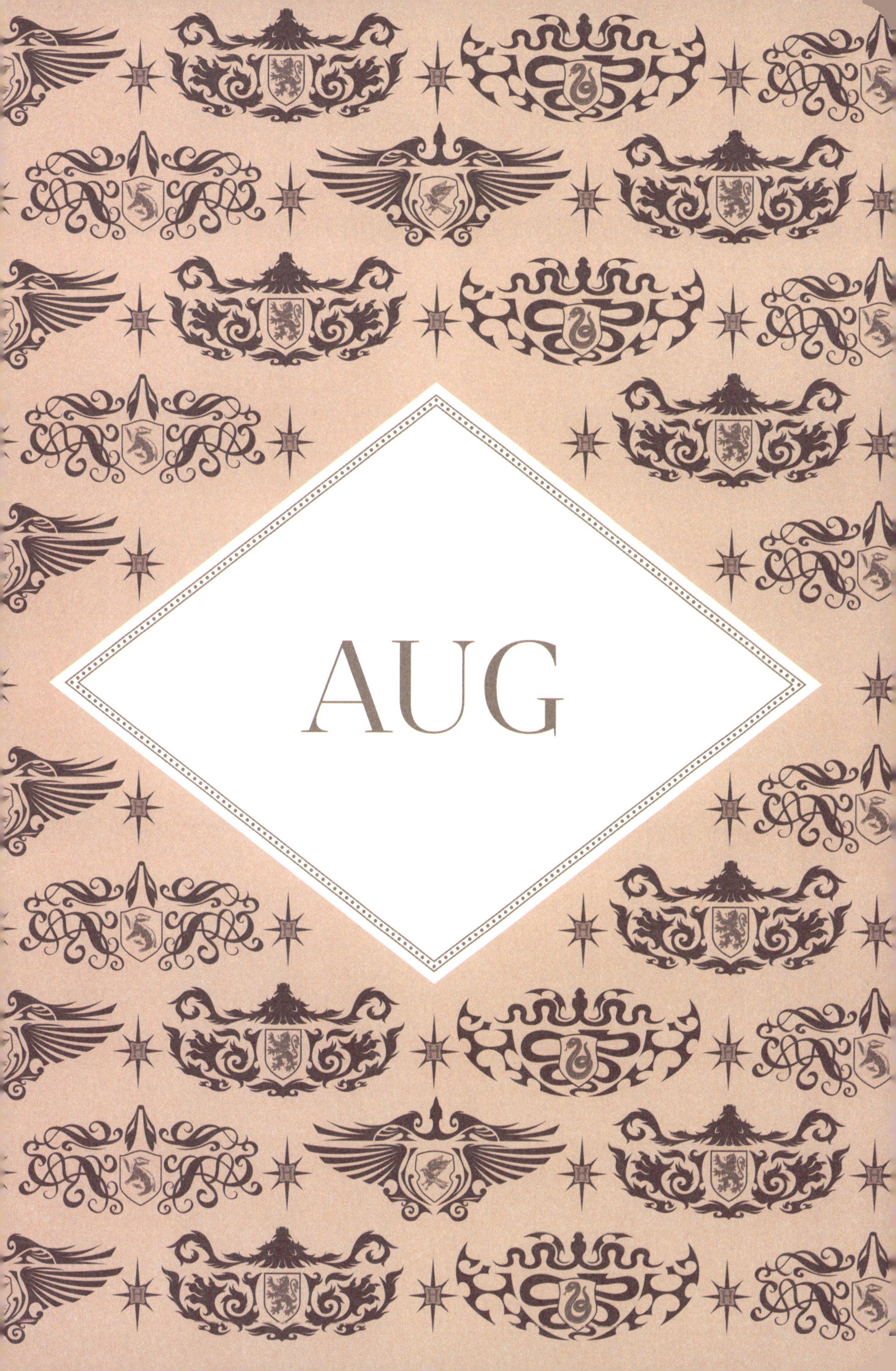
AUG

AUGUST 2023

SUNDAY	MONDAY	TUESDAY	WEDNESDAY
		1	2
6	7	8	9
13	14	15	16
20	21	22	23
27	28 Summer Bank Holiday (UK)	29	30

AUGUST 2023

THURSDAY	FRIDAY	SATURDAY	Notes
3	4	5	
10	11	12	
17	18	19	
24	25	26	
31			

31 Monday

HARRY POTTER'S BIRTHDAY

1 Tuesday

2 Wednesday

NOTES

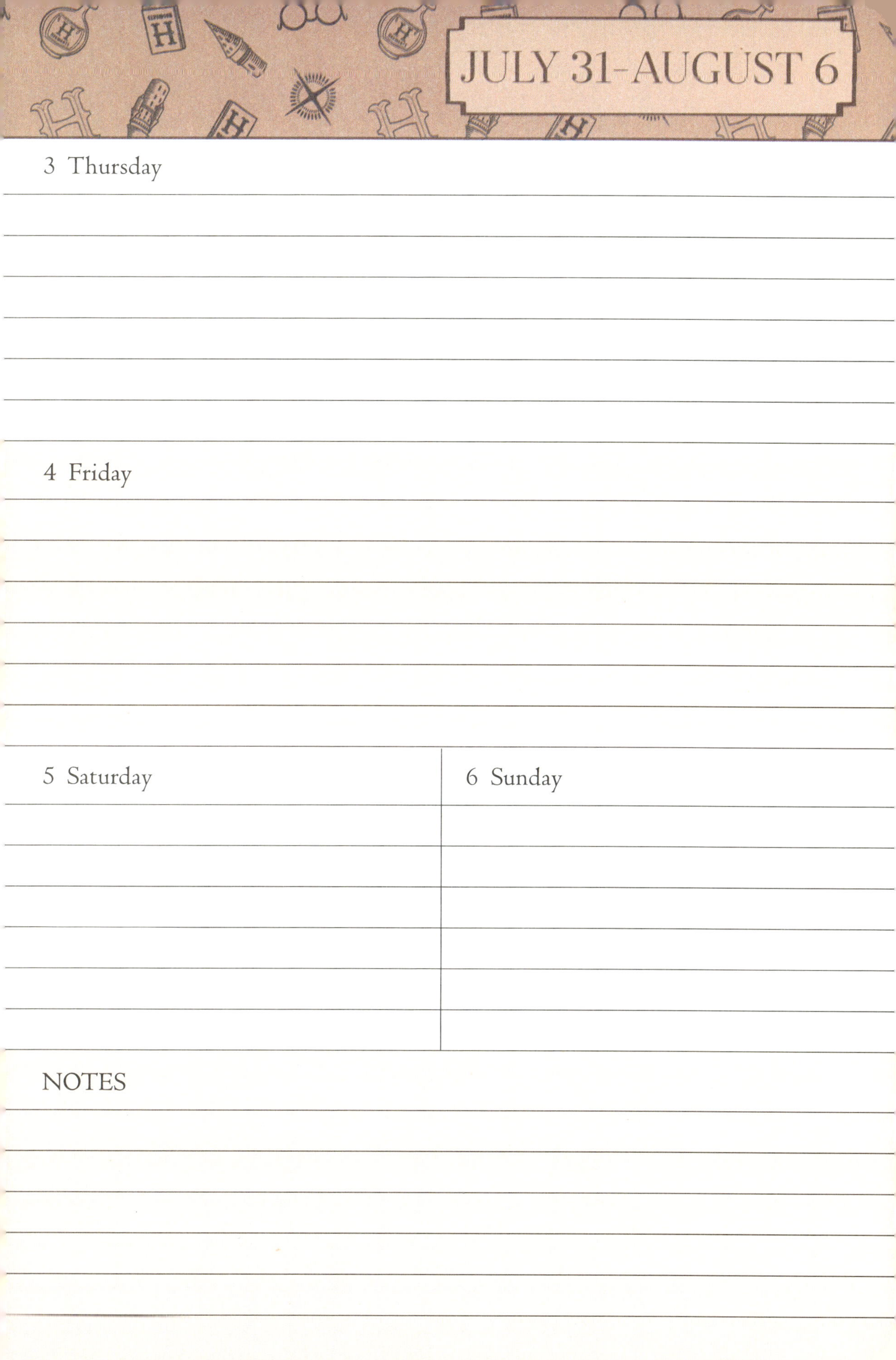

3 Thursday

4 Friday

5 Saturday

6 Sunday

NOTES

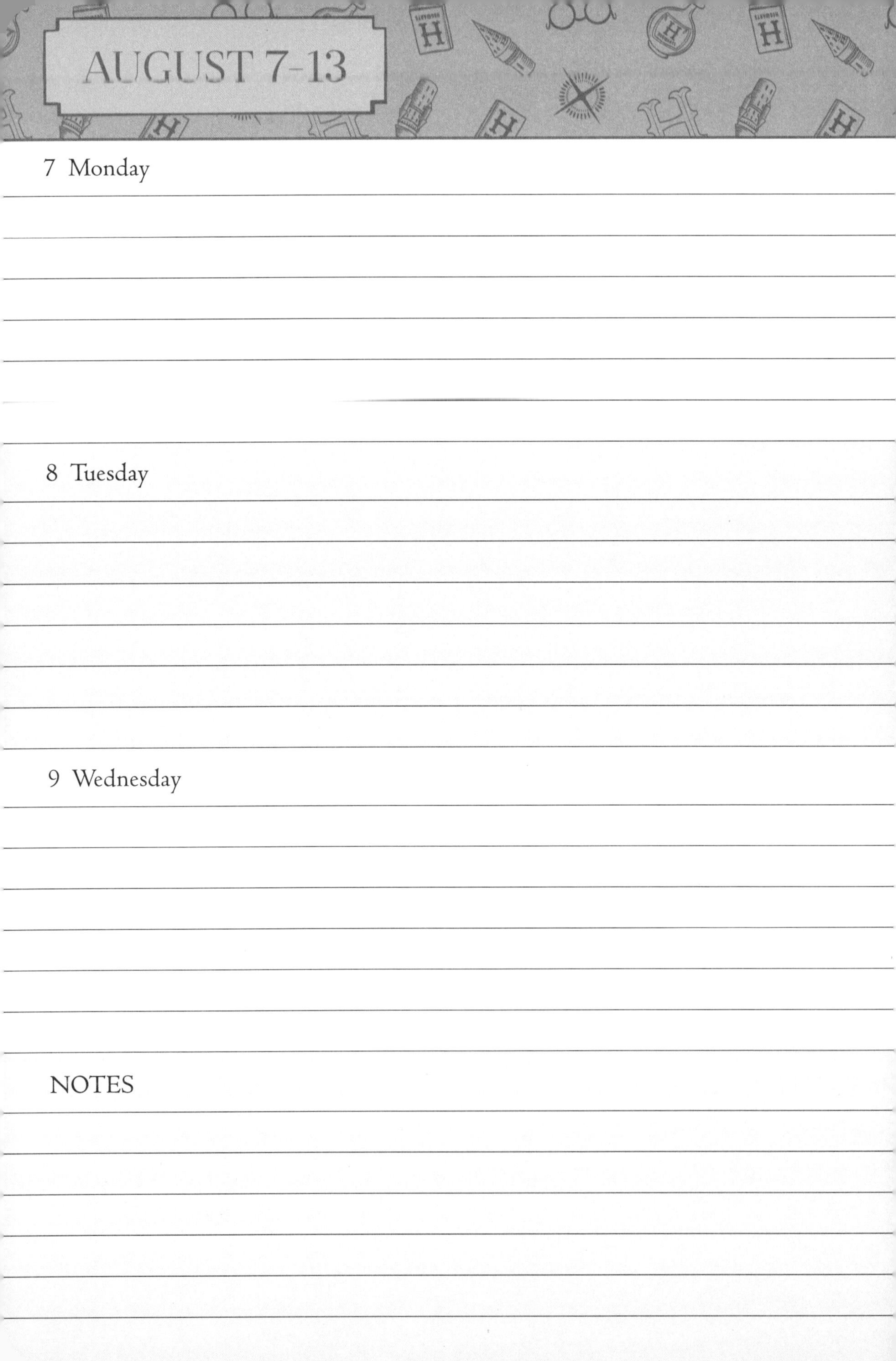

7 Monday

8 Tuesday

9 Wednesday

NOTES

10 Thursday

11 Friday

12 Saturday

13 Sunday

NOTES

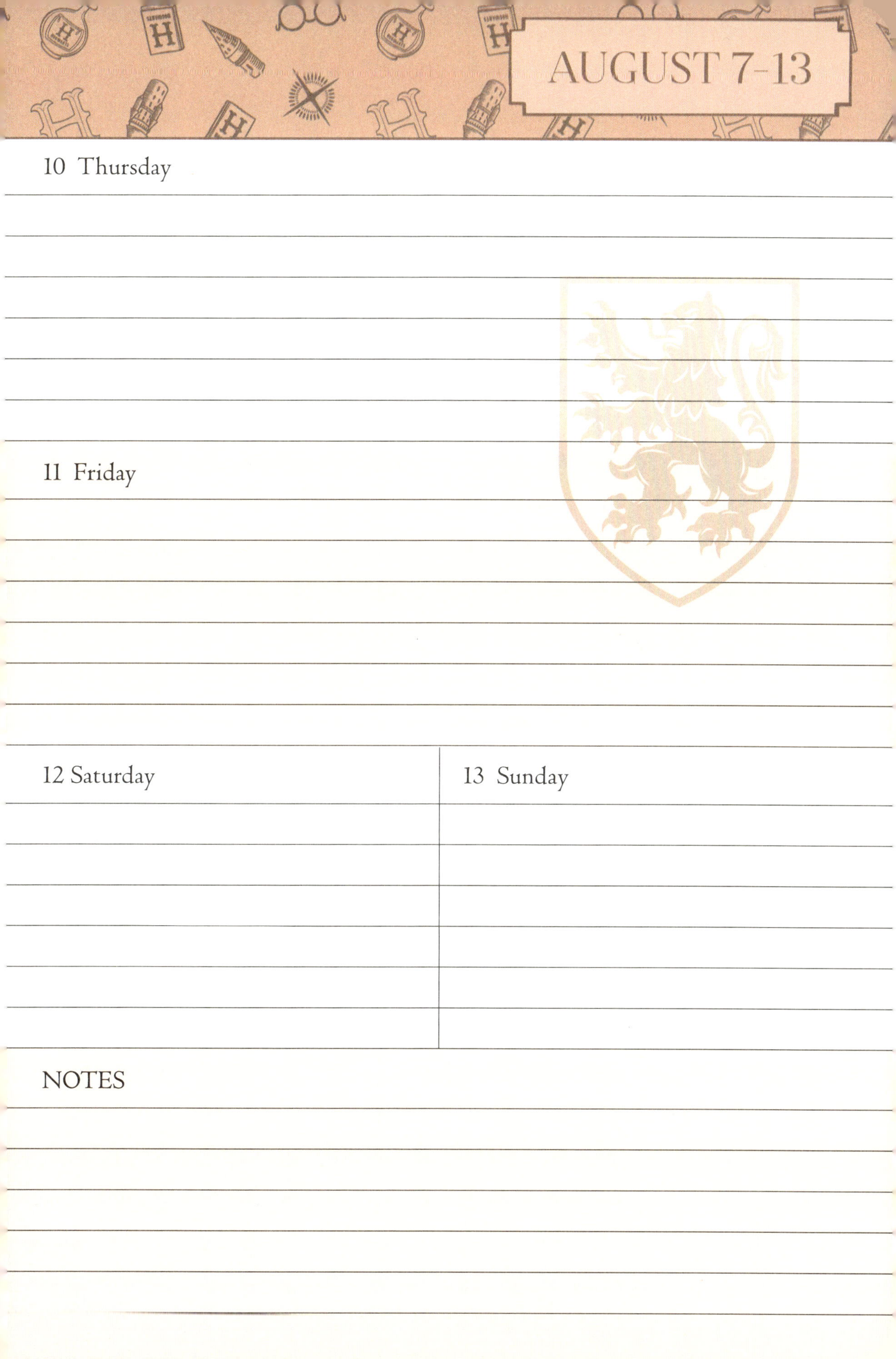

14 Monday

15 Tuesday

16 Wednesday

NOTES

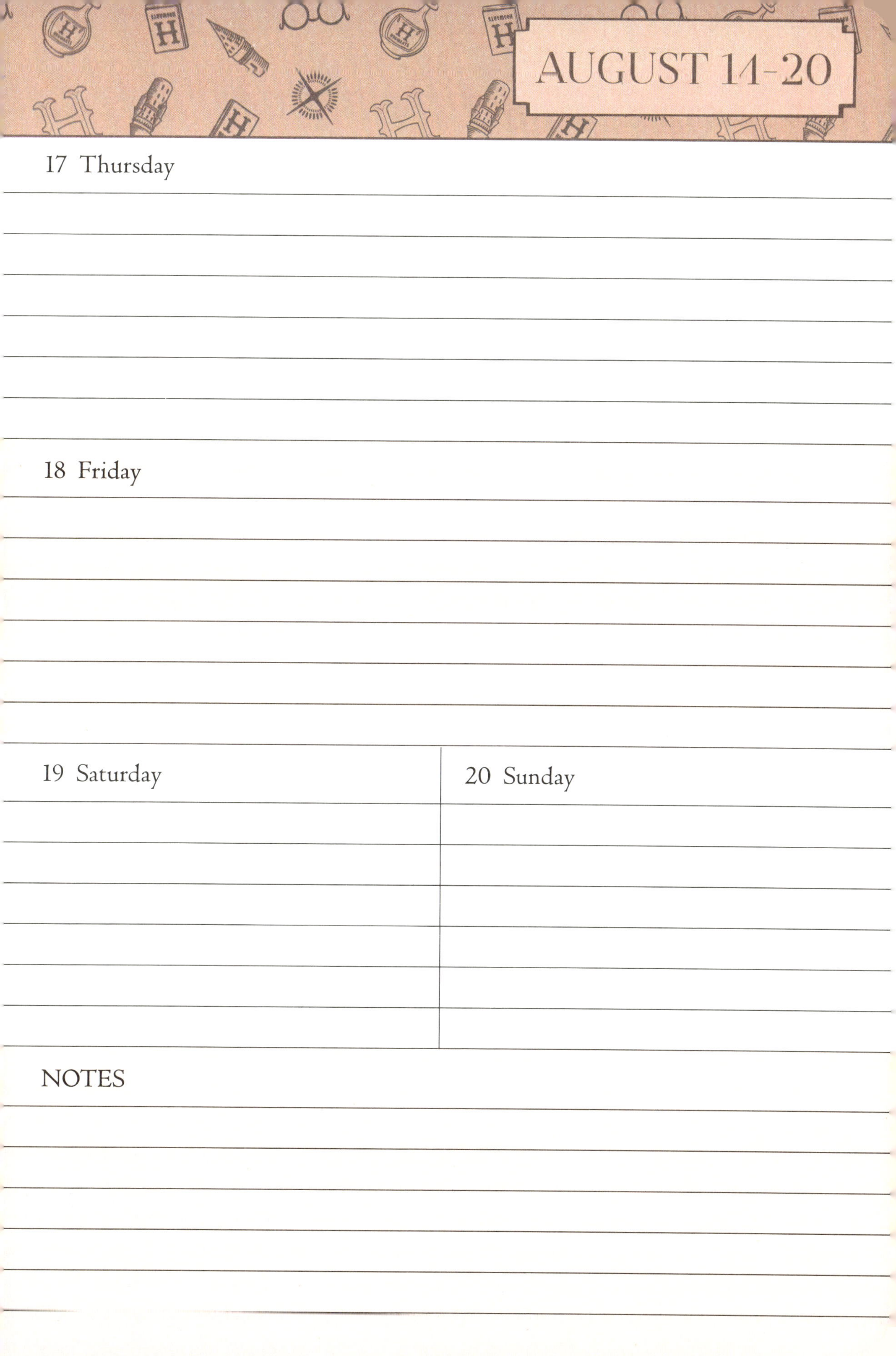

17 Thursday

18 Friday

19 Saturday

20 Sunday

NOTES

21 Monday

22 Tuesday

23 Wednesday

NOTES

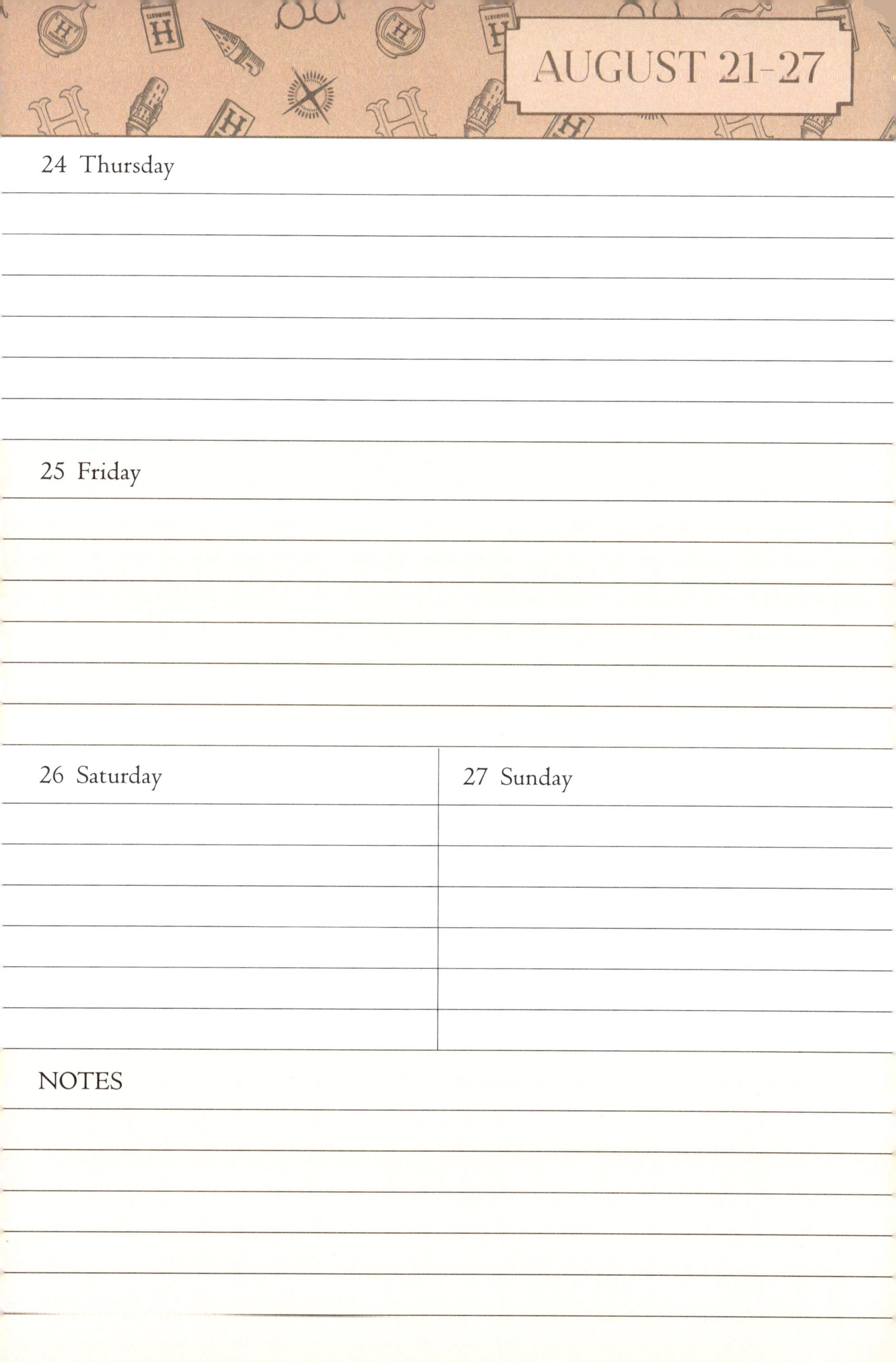

24 Thursday

25 Friday

26 Saturday

27 Sunday

NOTES

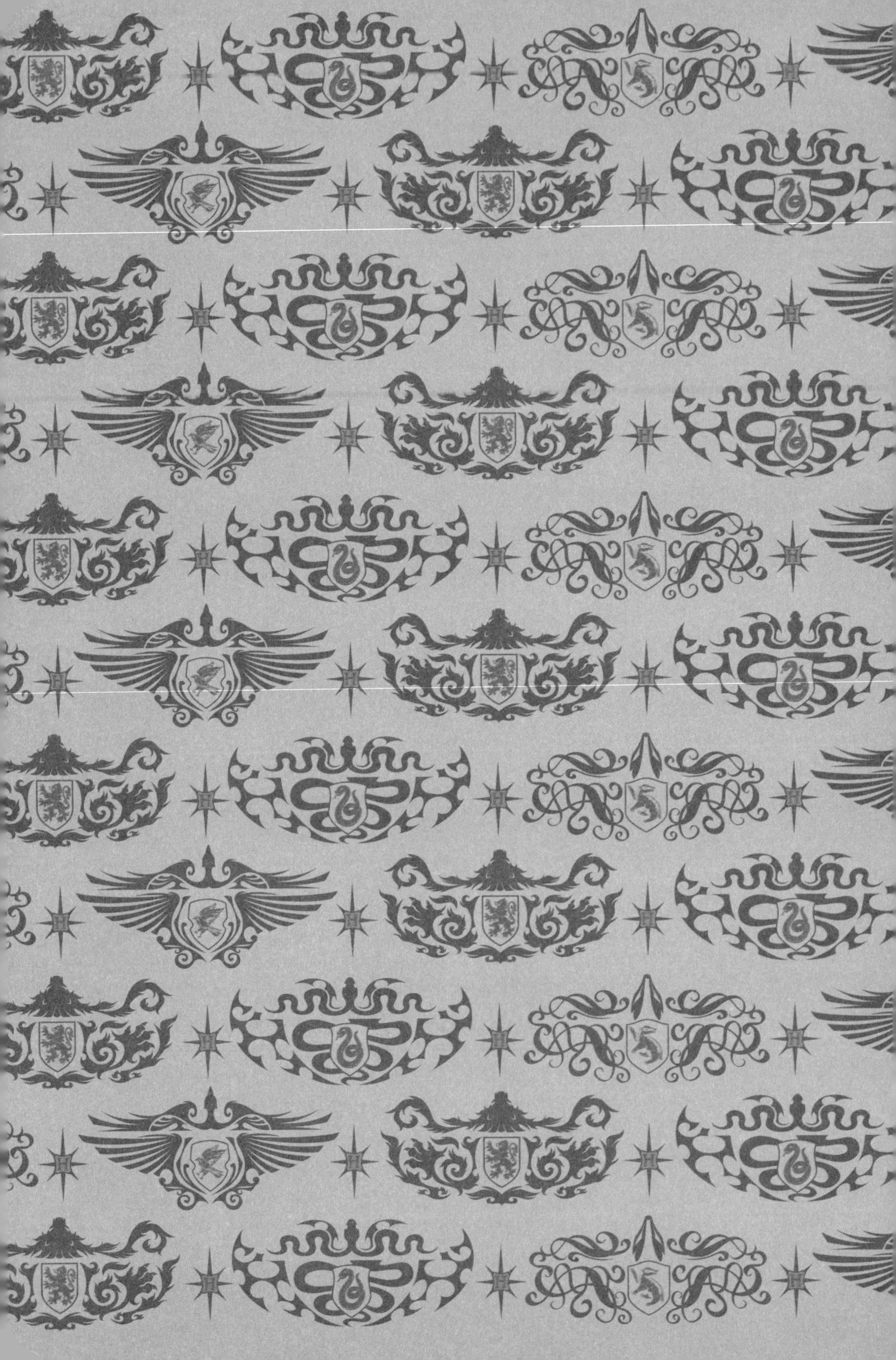

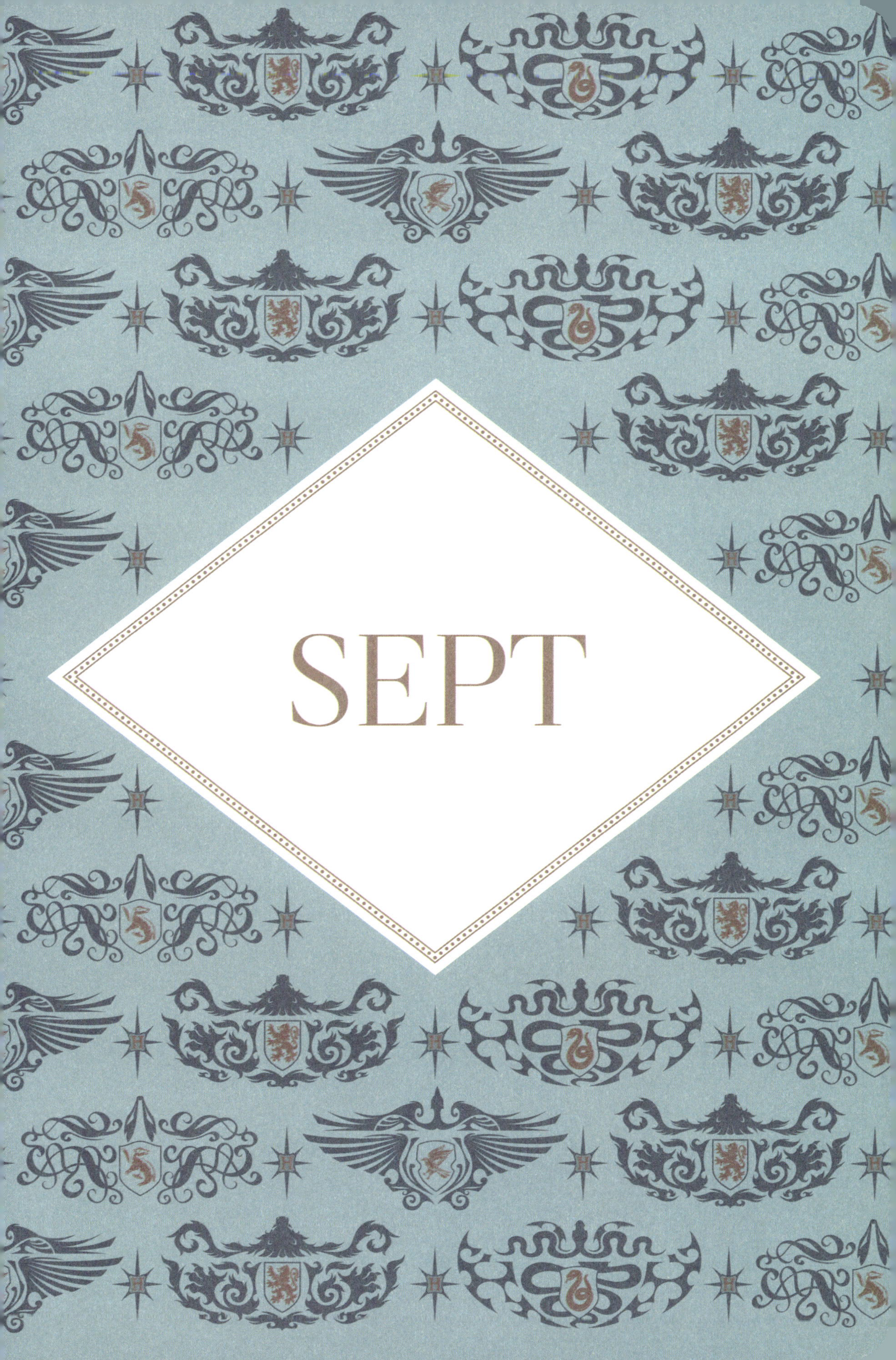
SEPT

SUNDAY	MONDAY	TUESDAY	WEDNESDAY
3	4	5	6
	Labor Day		
10	11	12	13
17	18	19	20
		Hermione Granger's Birthday	
24	25	26	27
Yom Kippur Begins at Sundown			

SEPTEMBER 2023

THURSDAY	FRIDAY	SATURDAY	Notes
	1	2	
7	8	9	
14	15 Rosh Hashanah Begins at Sundown	16	
21	22	23	
28	29	30	

AUGUST 28–SEPTEMBER 3

28 Monday   SUMMER BANK HOLIDAY (UK)

29 Tuesday

30 Wednesday

NOTES

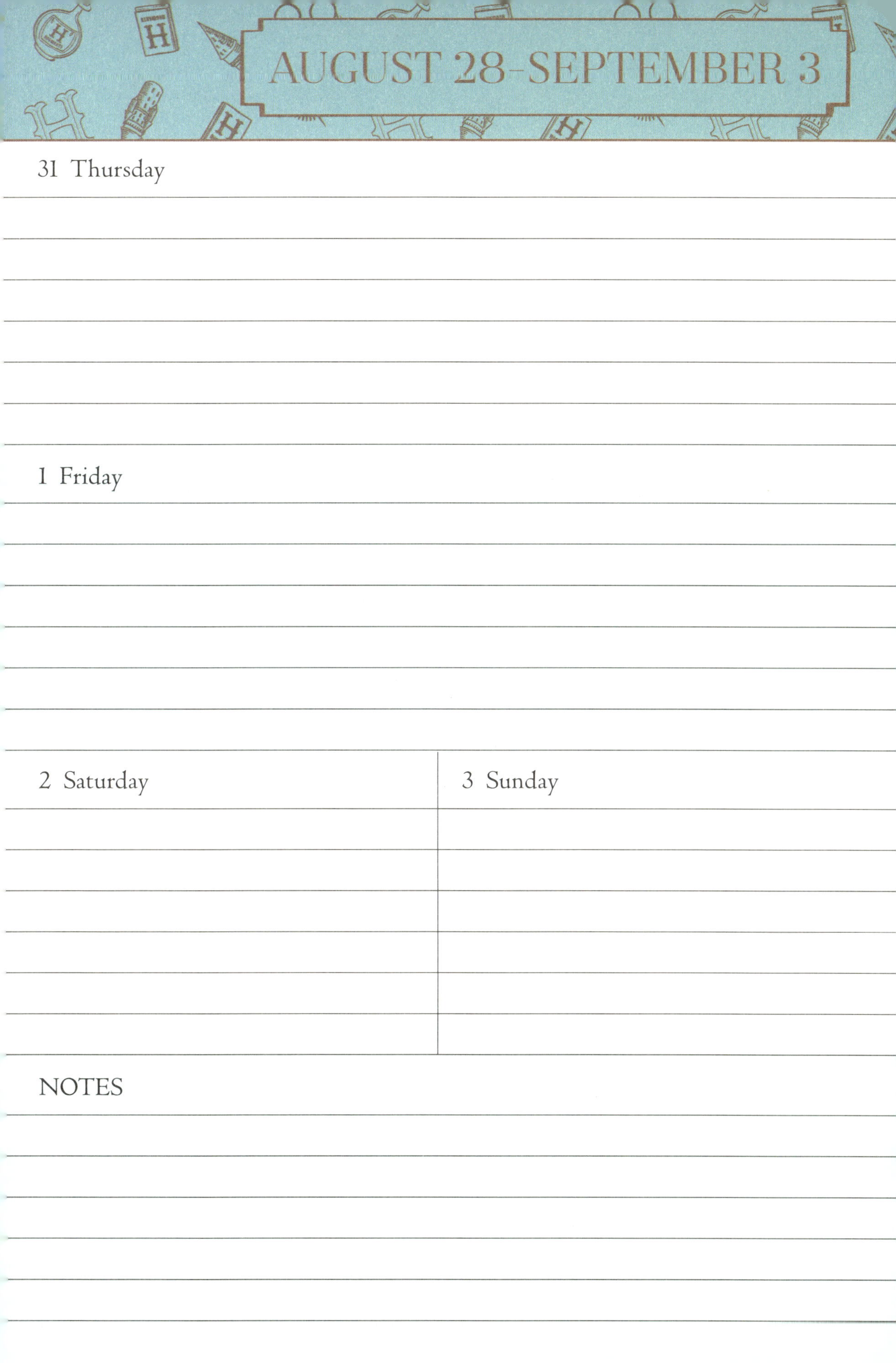

31 Thursday

1 Friday

2 Saturday

3 Sunday

NOTES

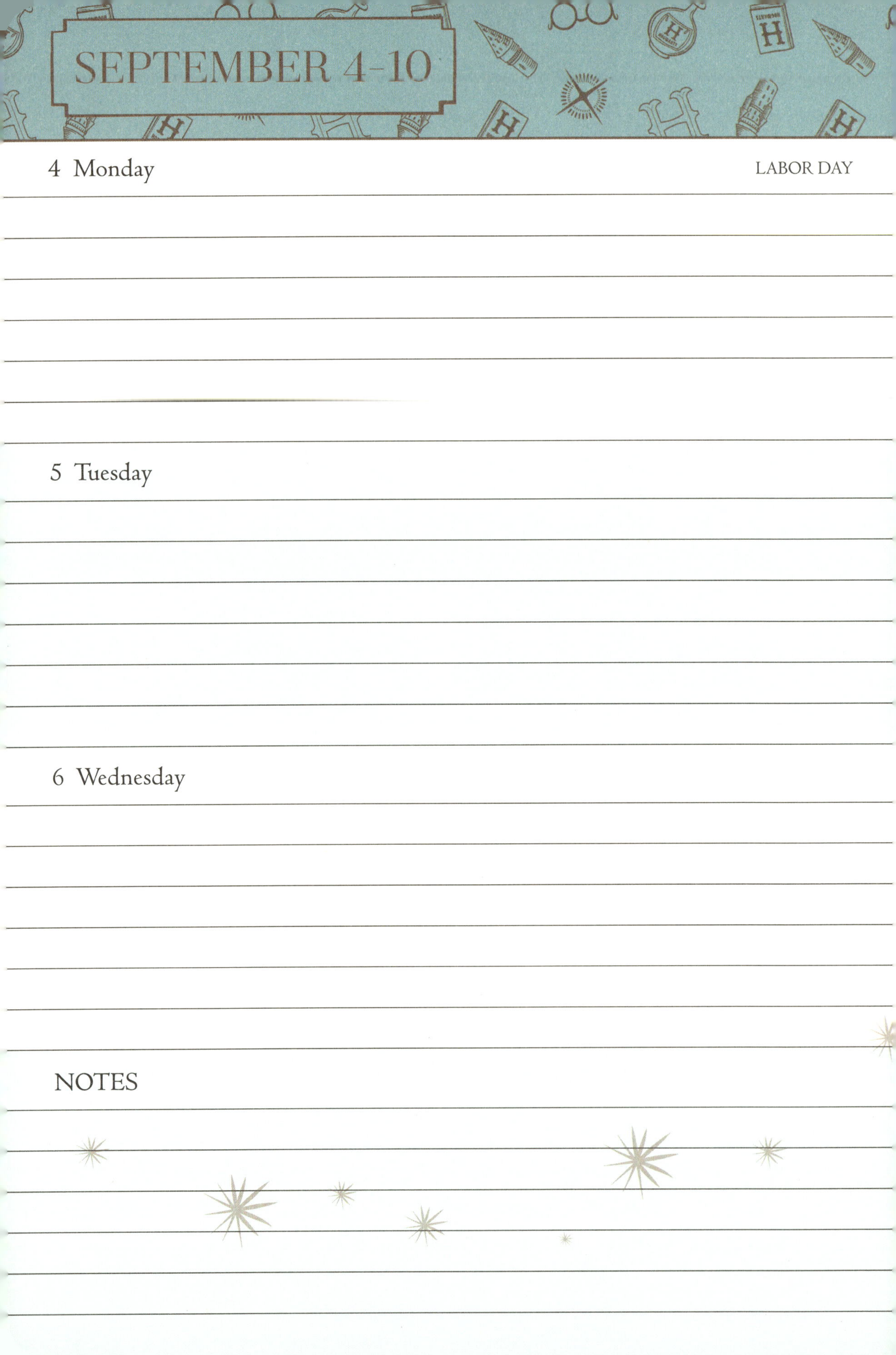

4 Monday

LABOR DAY

5 Tuesday

6 Wednesday

NOTES

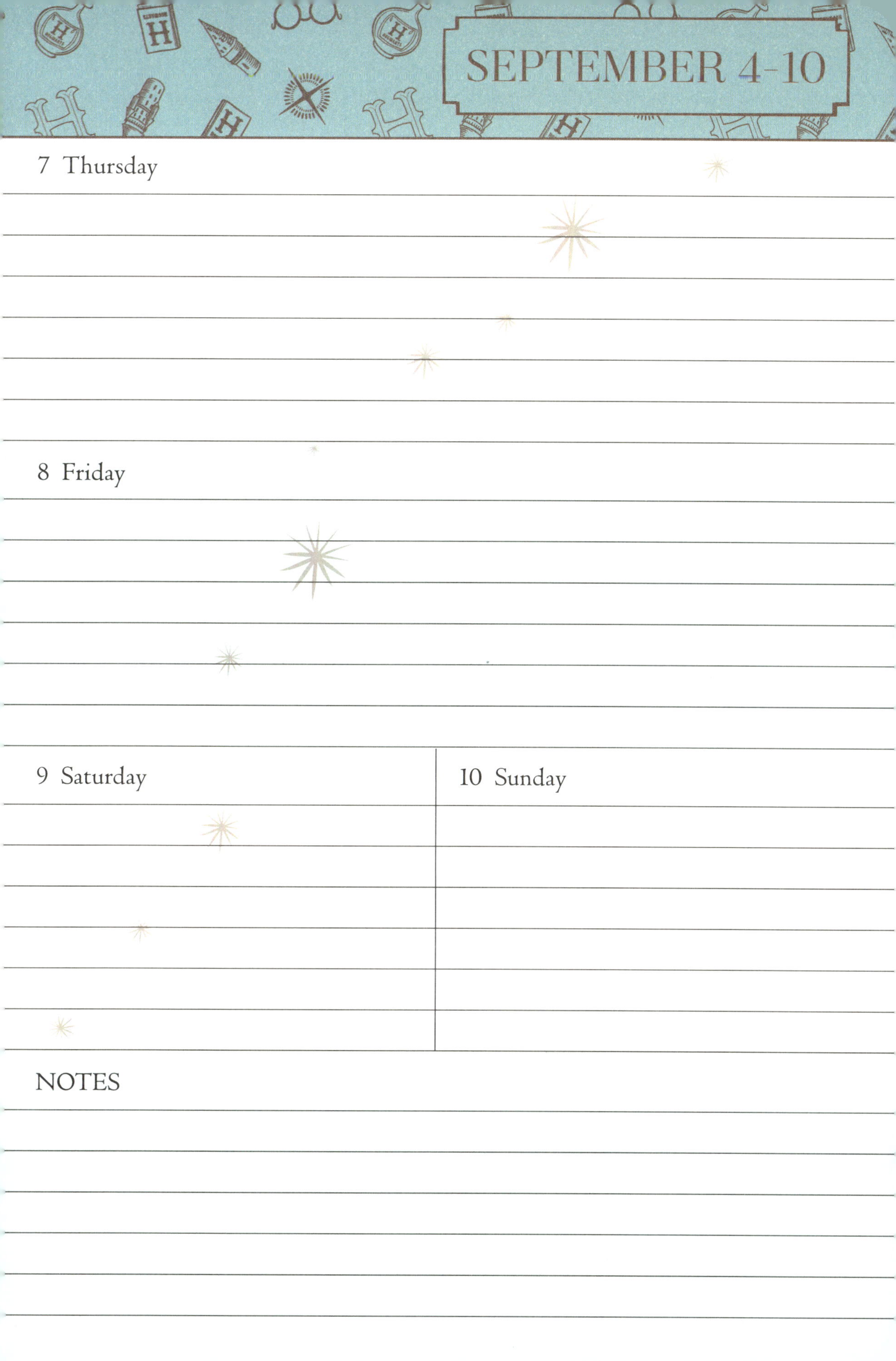

7 Thursday

8 Friday

9 Saturday

10 Sunday

NOTES

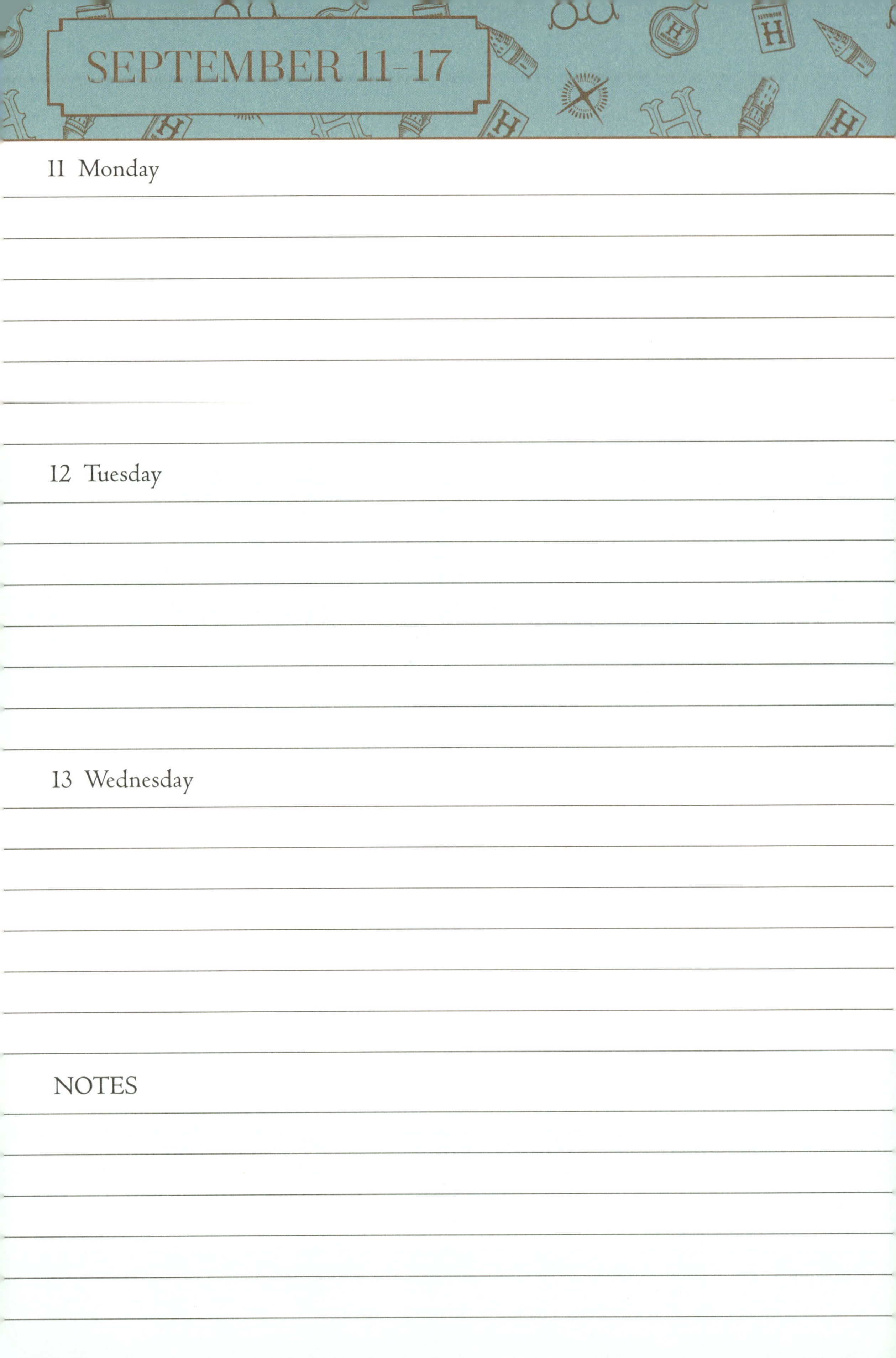

11 Monday

12 Tuesday

13 Wednesday

NOTES

14 Thursday

15 Friday   ROSH HASHANAH BEGINS AT SUNDOWN

16 Saturday

17 Sunday

NOTES

18 Monday

19 Tuesday   HERMIONE GRANGER'S BIRTHDAY

20 Wednesday

NOTES

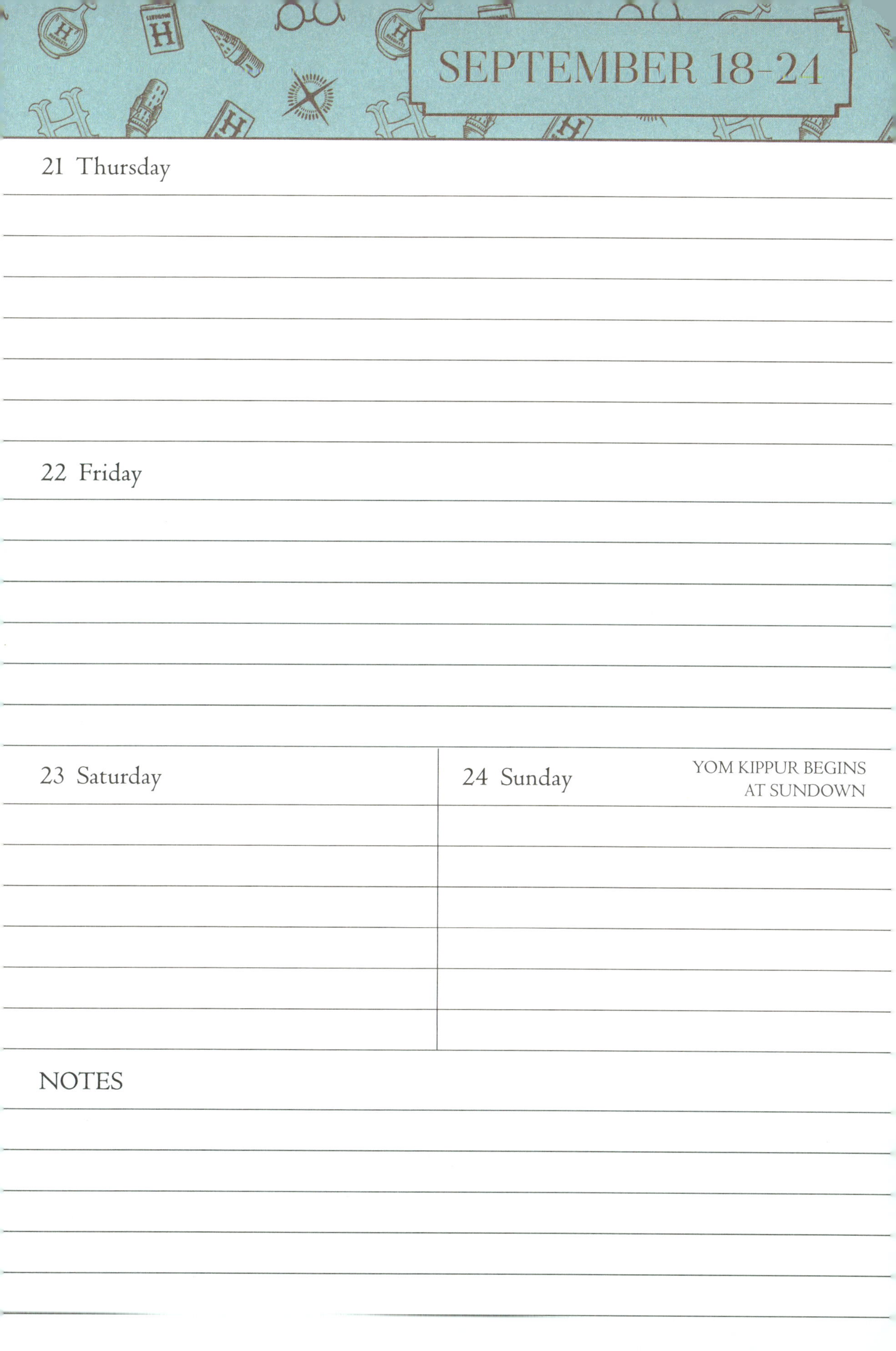

21 Thursday

22 Friday

23 Saturday

24 Sunday

YOM KIPPUR BEGINS
AT SUNDOWN

NOTES

25 Monday

26 Tuesday

27 Wednesday

NOTES

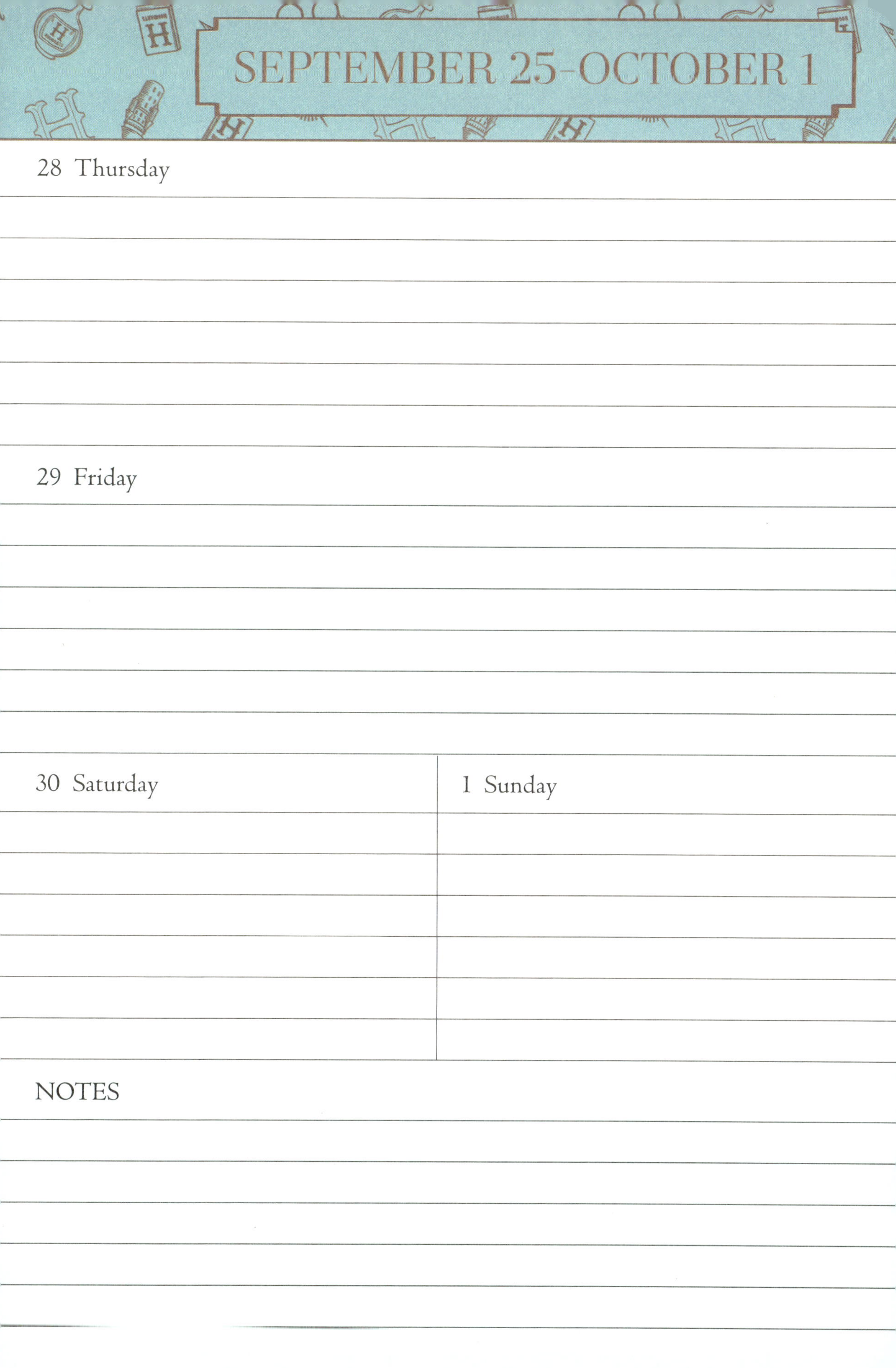

28 Thursday

29 Friday

30 Saturday

1 Sunday

NOTES

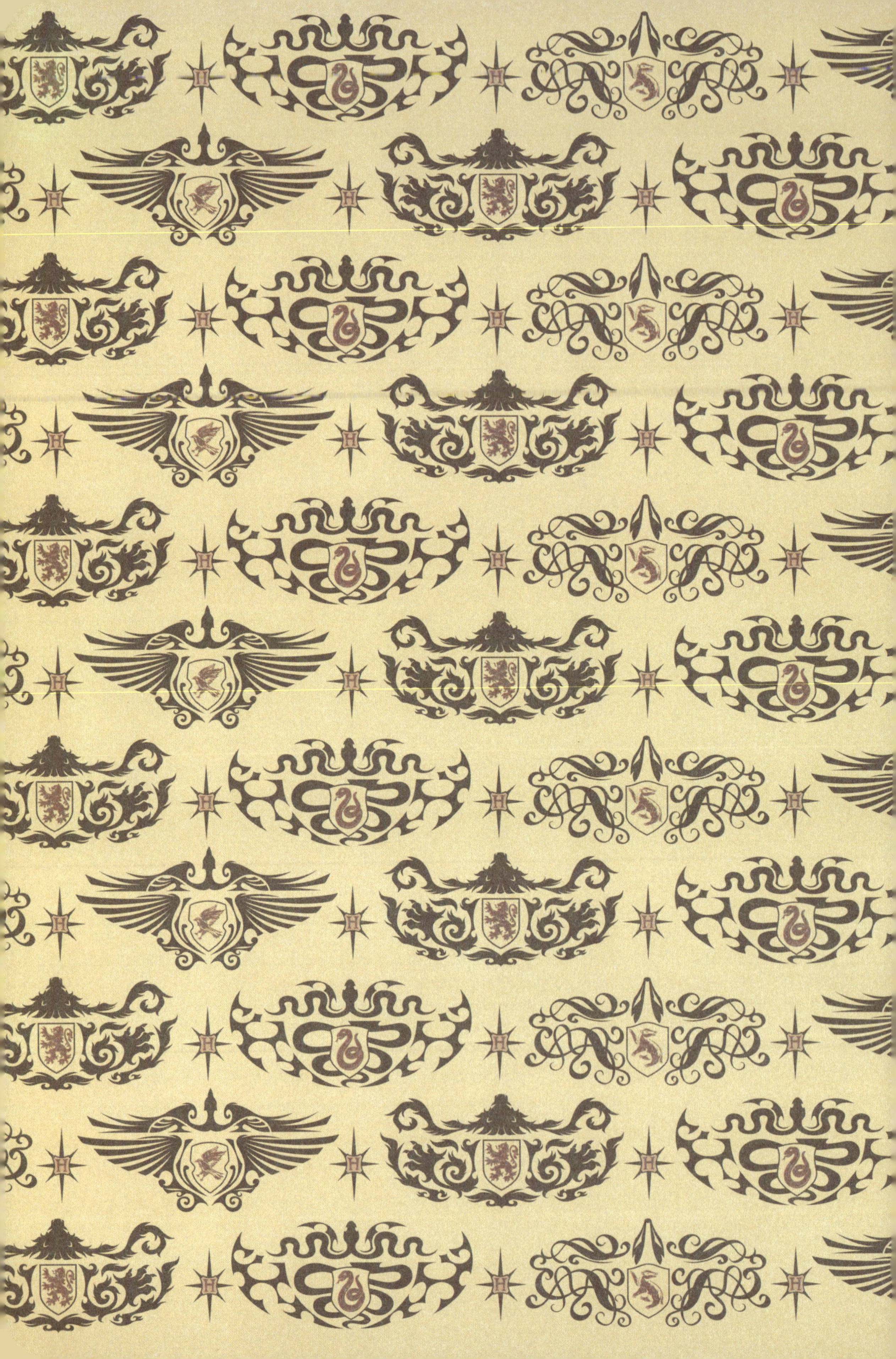

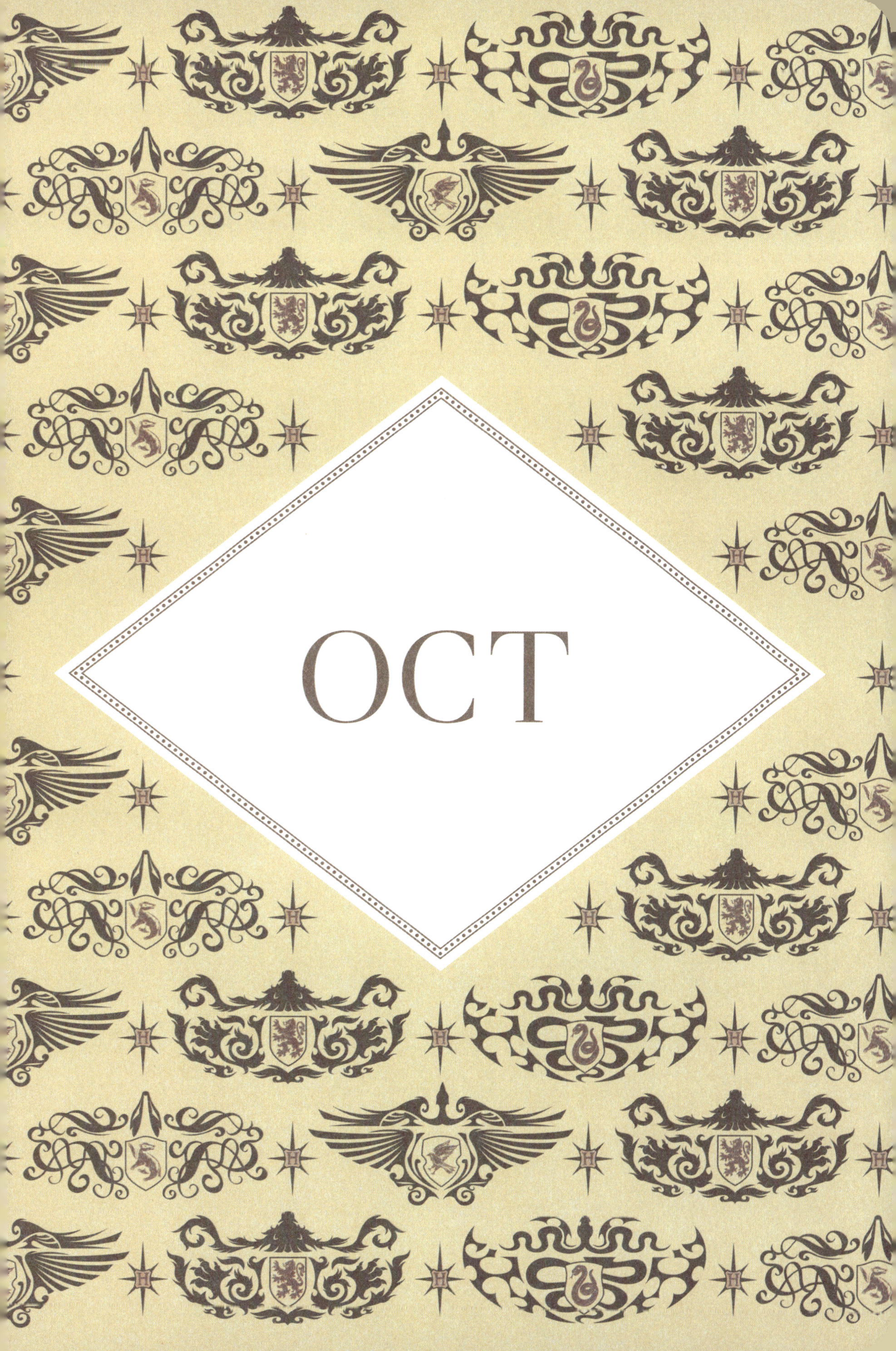
OCT

OCTOBER 2023

SUNDAY	MONDAY	TUESDAY	WEDNESDAY
1	2	3	4
8	9 Columbus Day Indigenous Peoples' Day	10	11
15	16	17	18
22	23	24	25
29	30	31 Halloween	

THURSDAY	FRIDAY	SATURDAY	Notes
5	6	7	
12	13	14	
19	20	21	
26	27	28	

2 Monday

3 Tuesday

4 Wednesday

NOTES

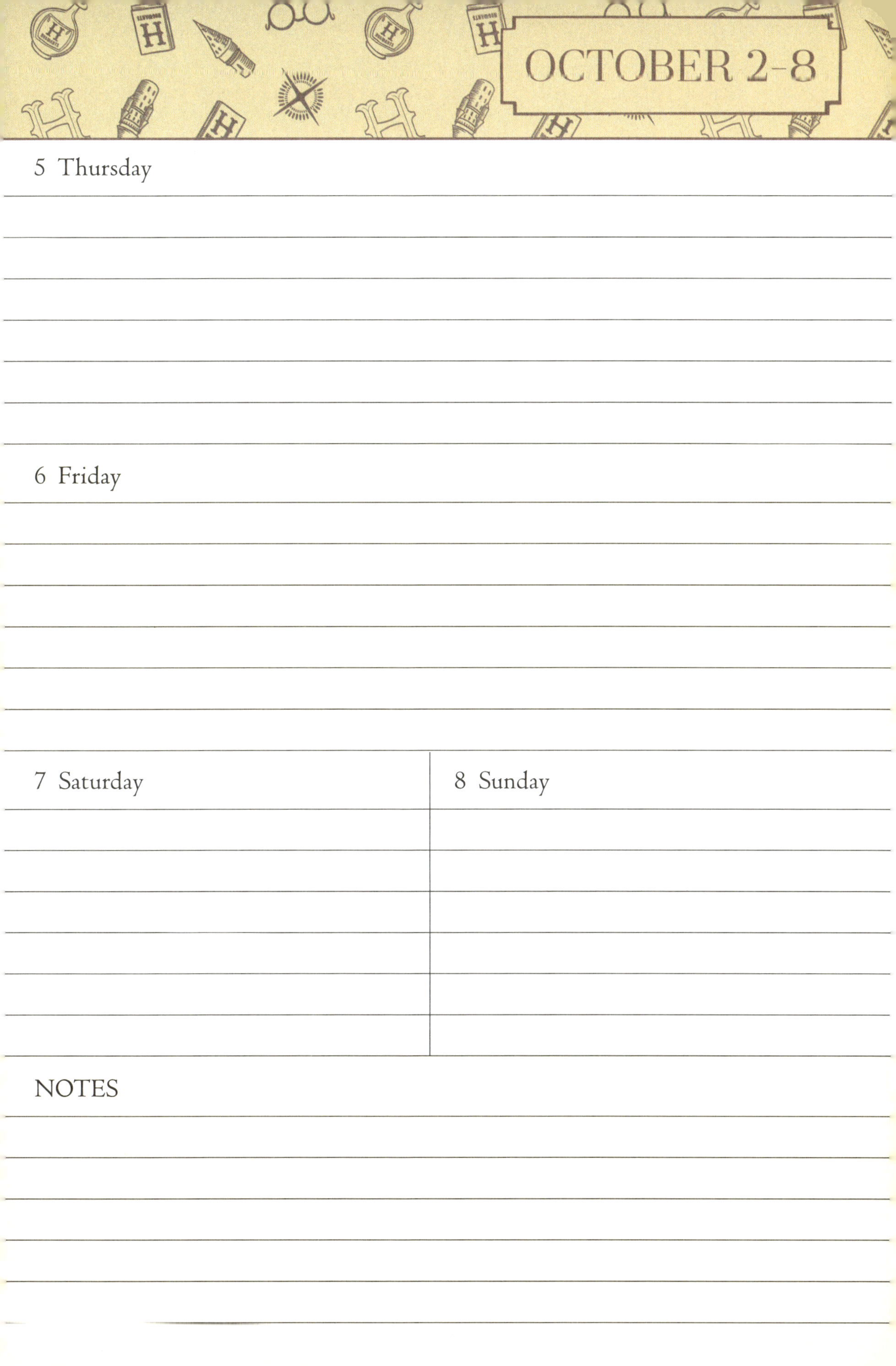

5 Thursday

6 Friday

7 Saturday

8 Sunday

NOTES

OCTOBER 9–15

9 Monday

10 Tuesday

11 Wednesday

NOTES

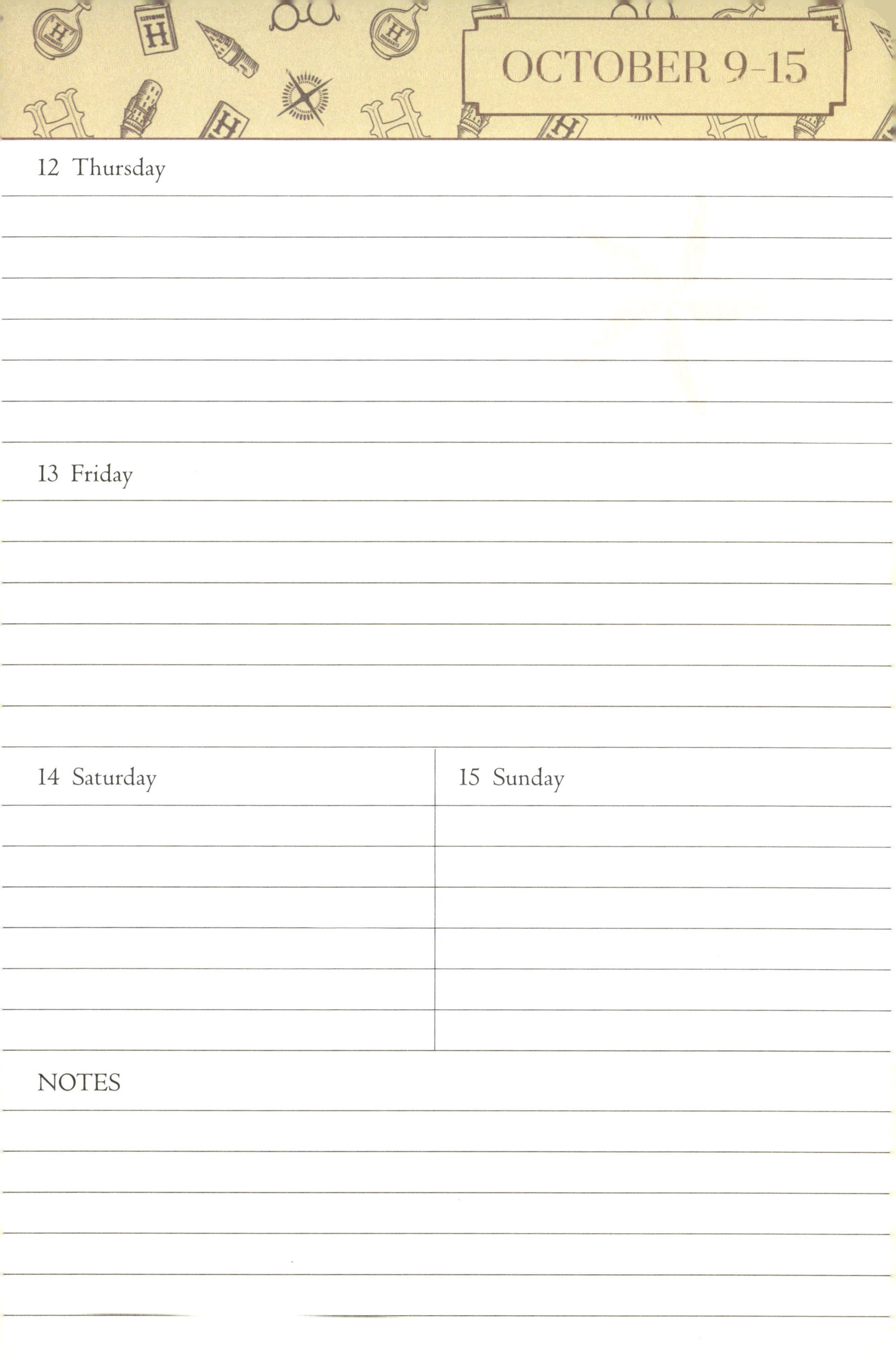

12 Thursday

13 Friday

14 Saturday

15 Sunday

NOTES

16 Monday

17 Tuesday

18 Wednesday

NOTES

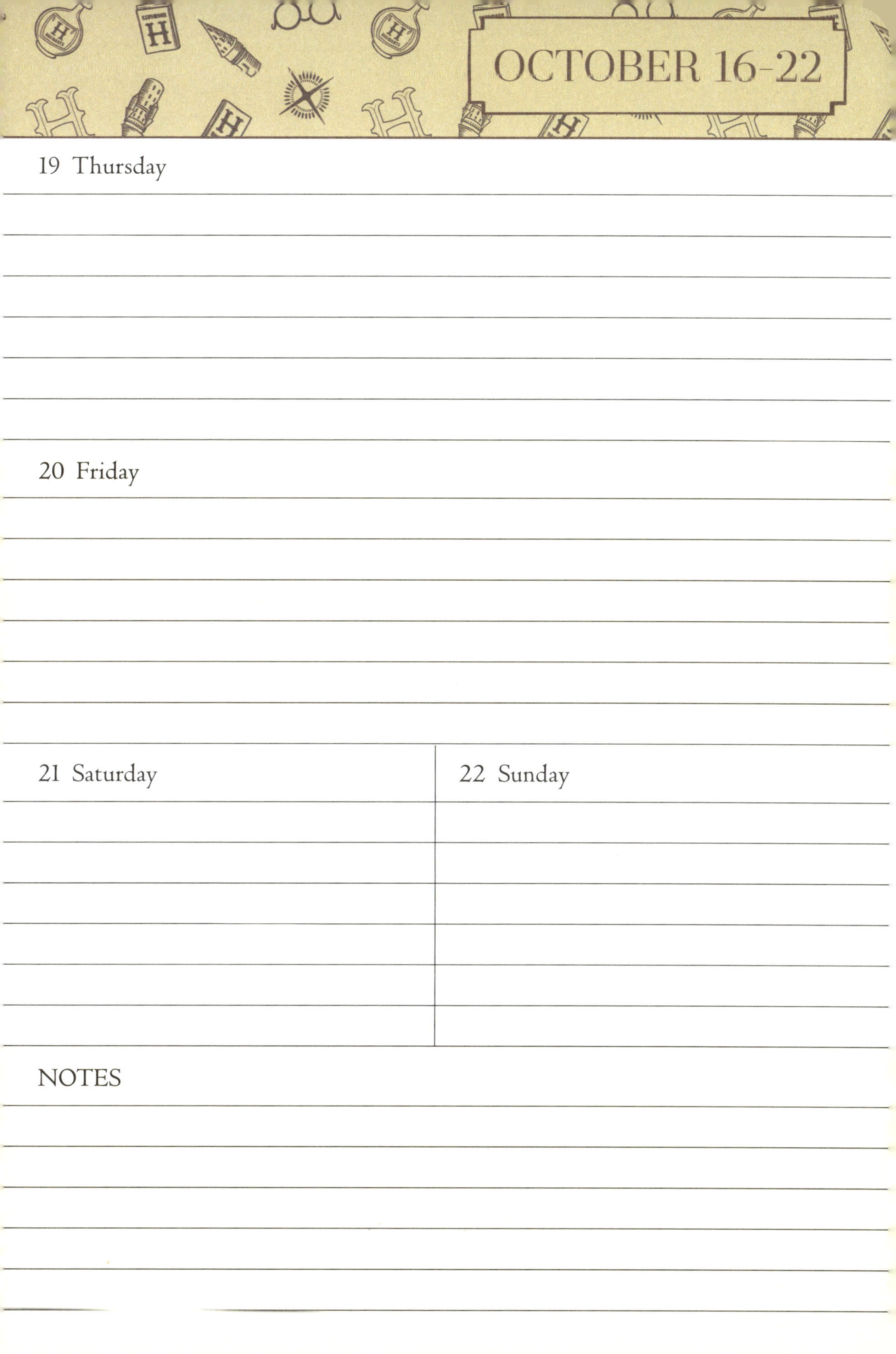

19 Thursday

20 Friday

21 Saturday

22 Sunday

NOTES

23 Monday

24 Tuesday

25 Wednesday

NOTES

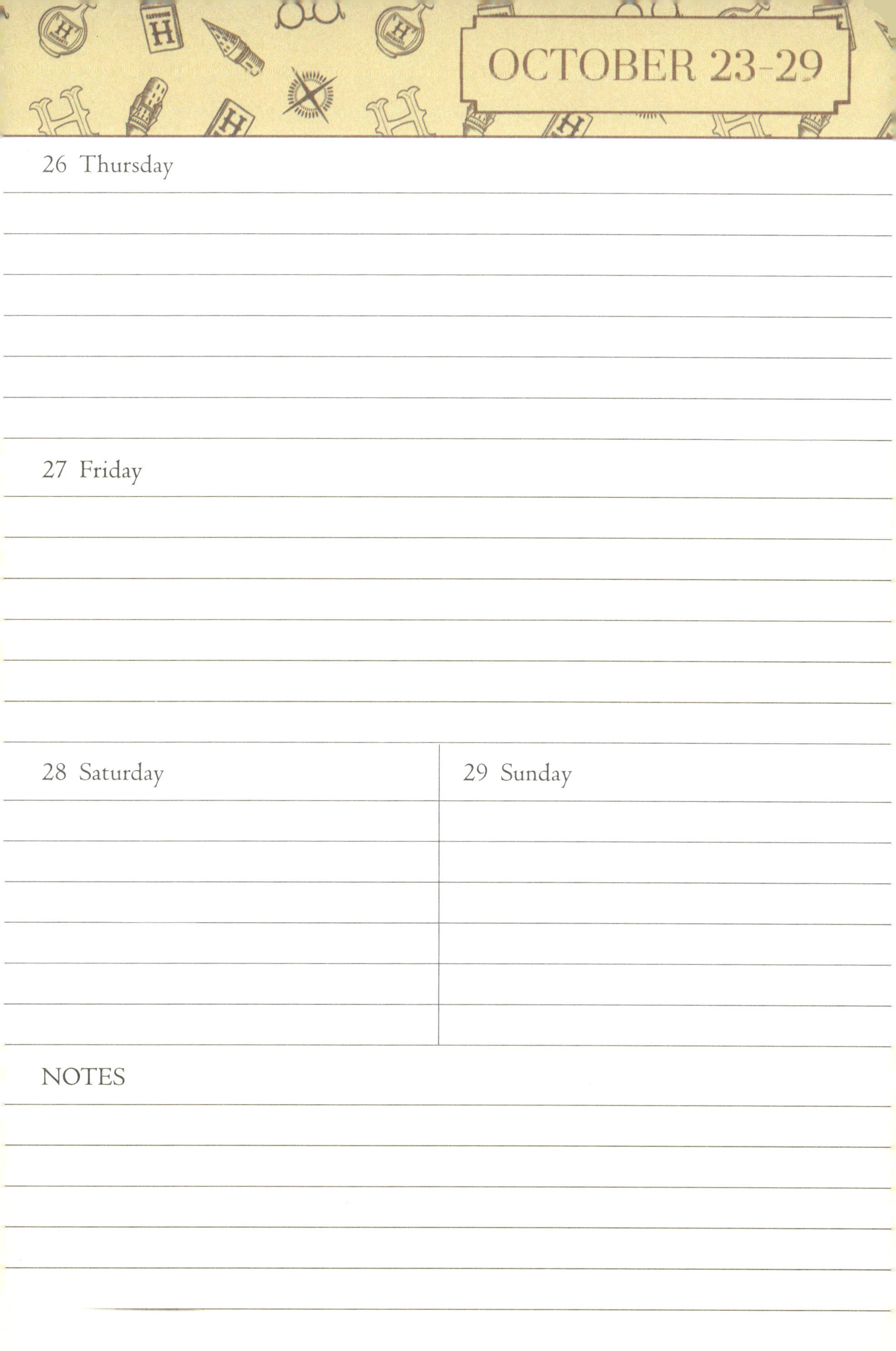

26 Thursday

27 Friday

28 Saturday

29 Sunday

NOTES

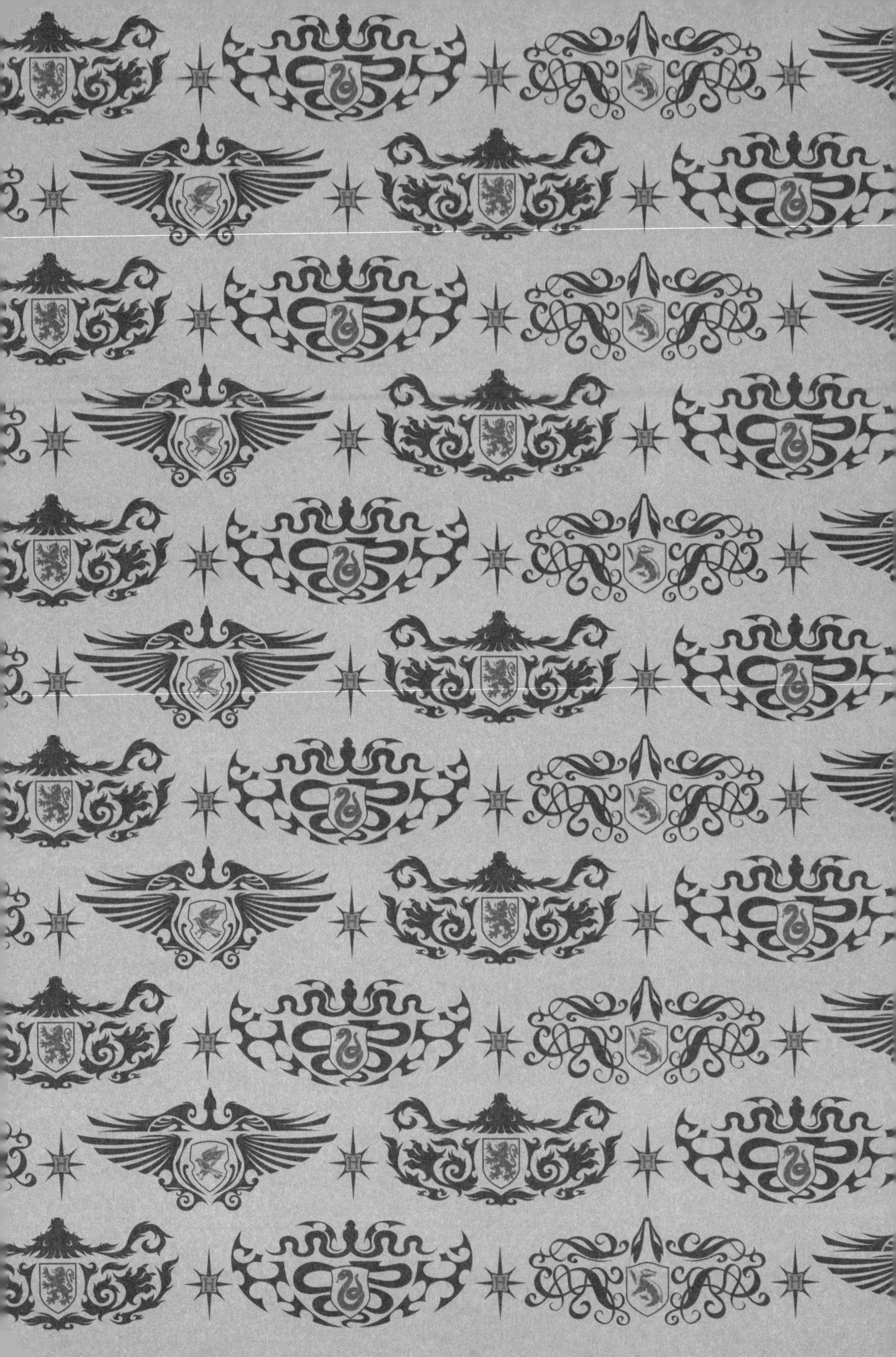

NOV

NOVEMBER 2023

SUNDAY	MONDAY	TUESDAY	WEDNESDAY
			1
5 Daylight Savings Time Ends	6	7	8
12	13	14	15
19	20	21	22
26	27	28	29

THURSDAY	FRIDAY	SATURDAY	Notes
2	3	4	
9	10	11 Veterans Day	
16	17	18	
23 Thanksgiving Day	24	25	
30			

30 Monday

31 Tuesday   HALLOWEEN

1 Wednesday

NOTES

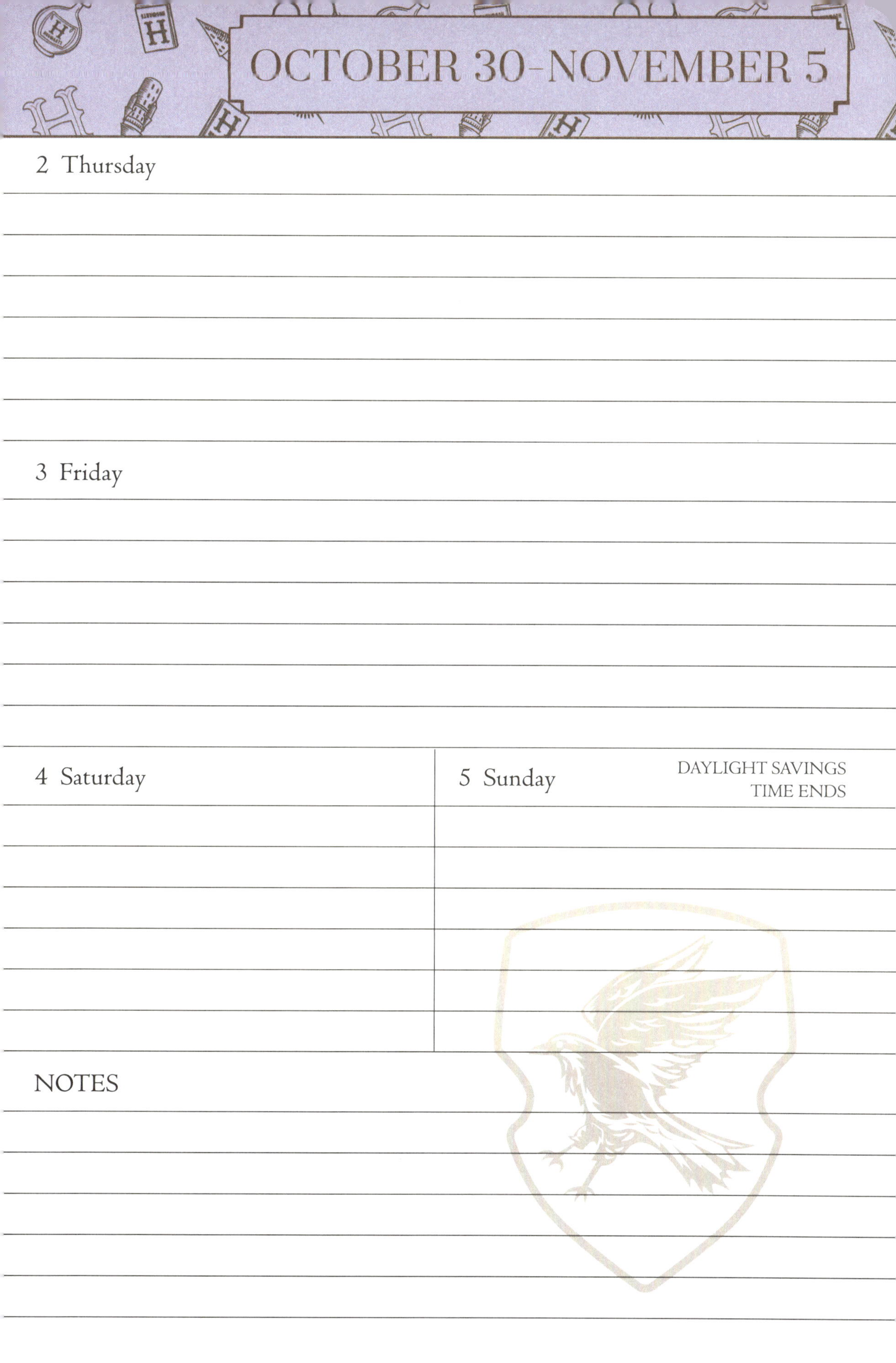

2 Thursday

3 Friday

4 Saturday

5 Sunday — DAYLIGHT SAVINGS TIME ENDS

NOTES

6 Monday

7 Tuesday

8 Wednesday

NOTES

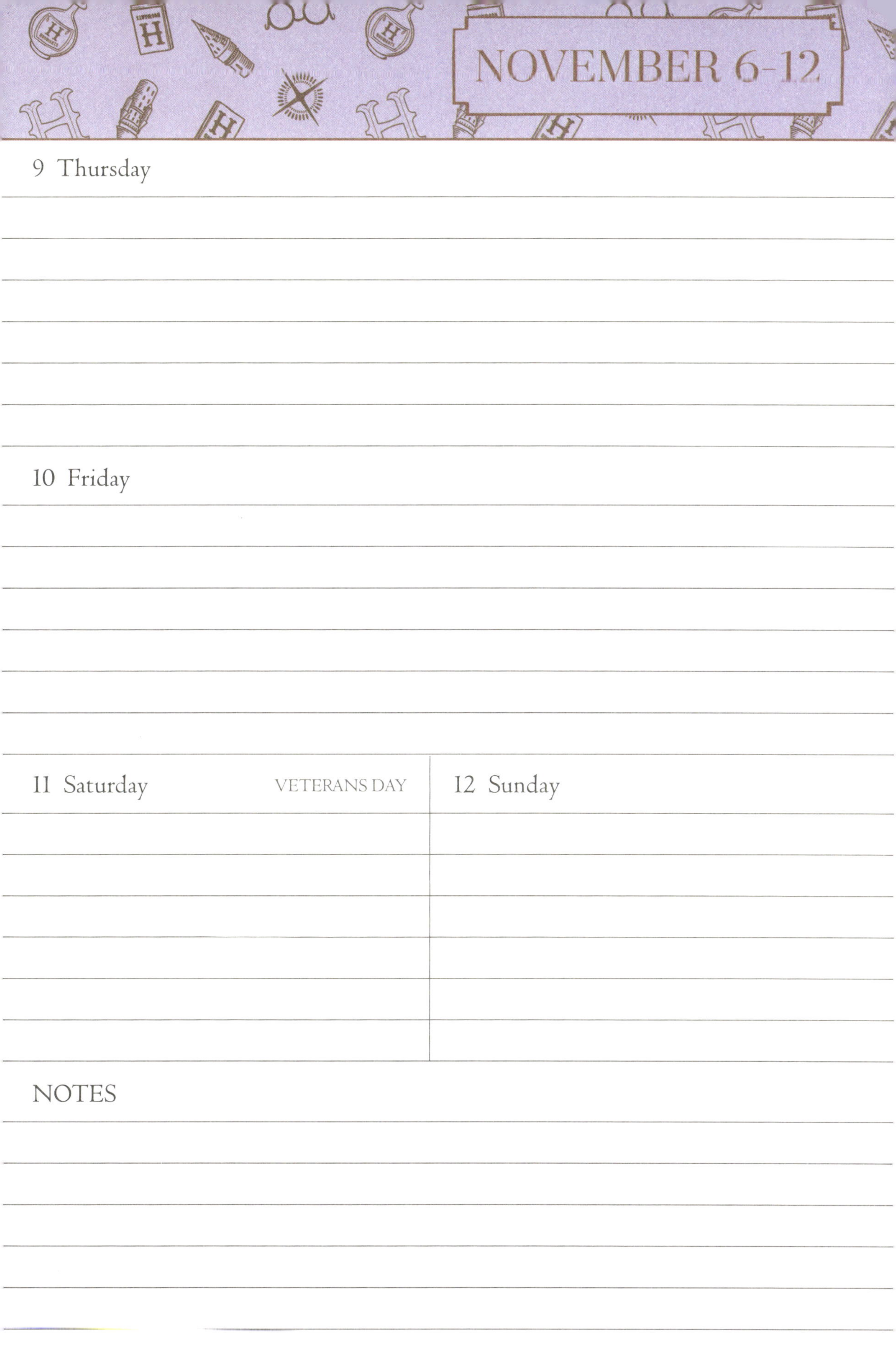

9 Thursday

10 Friday

11 Saturday VETERANS DAY

12 Sunday

NOTES

13 Monday

14 Tuesday

15 Wednesday

NOTES

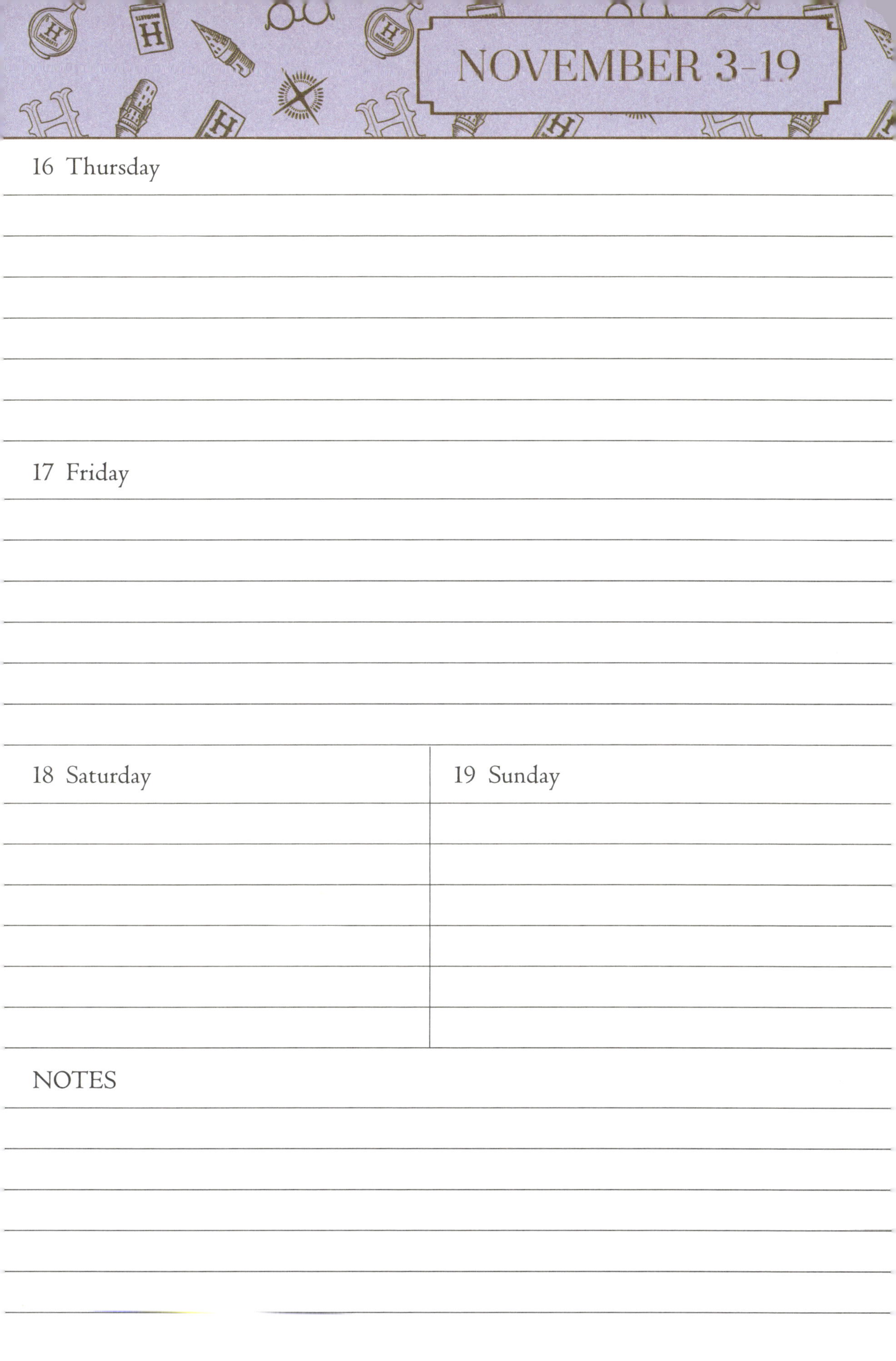

16 Thursday

17 Friday

18 Saturday

19 Sunday

NOTES

20 Monday

21 Tuesday

22 Wednesday

NOTES

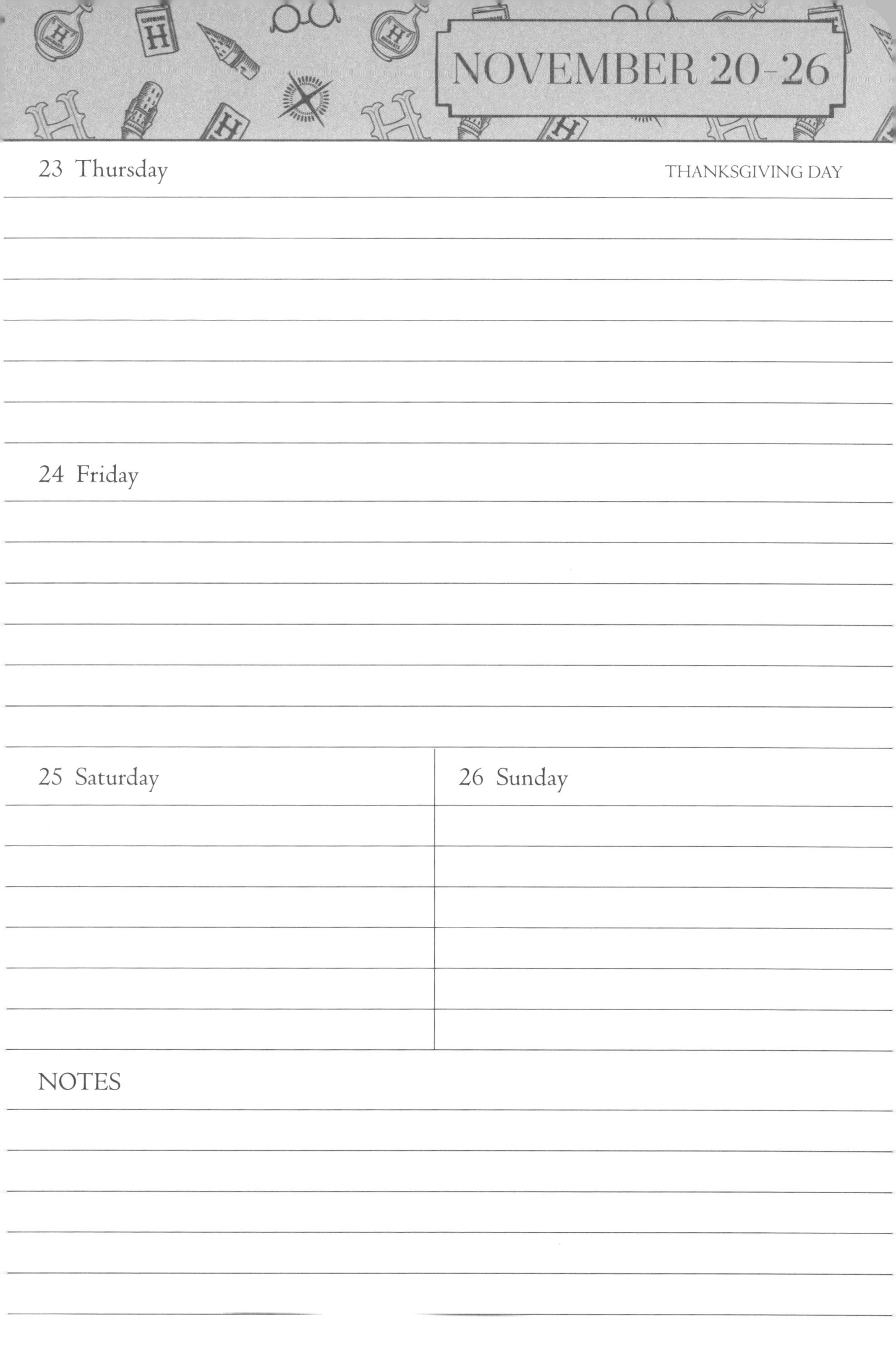

23 Thursday

THANKSGIVING DAY

24 Friday

25 Saturday

26 Sunday

NOTES

27 Monday

28 Tuesday

29 Wednesday

NOTES

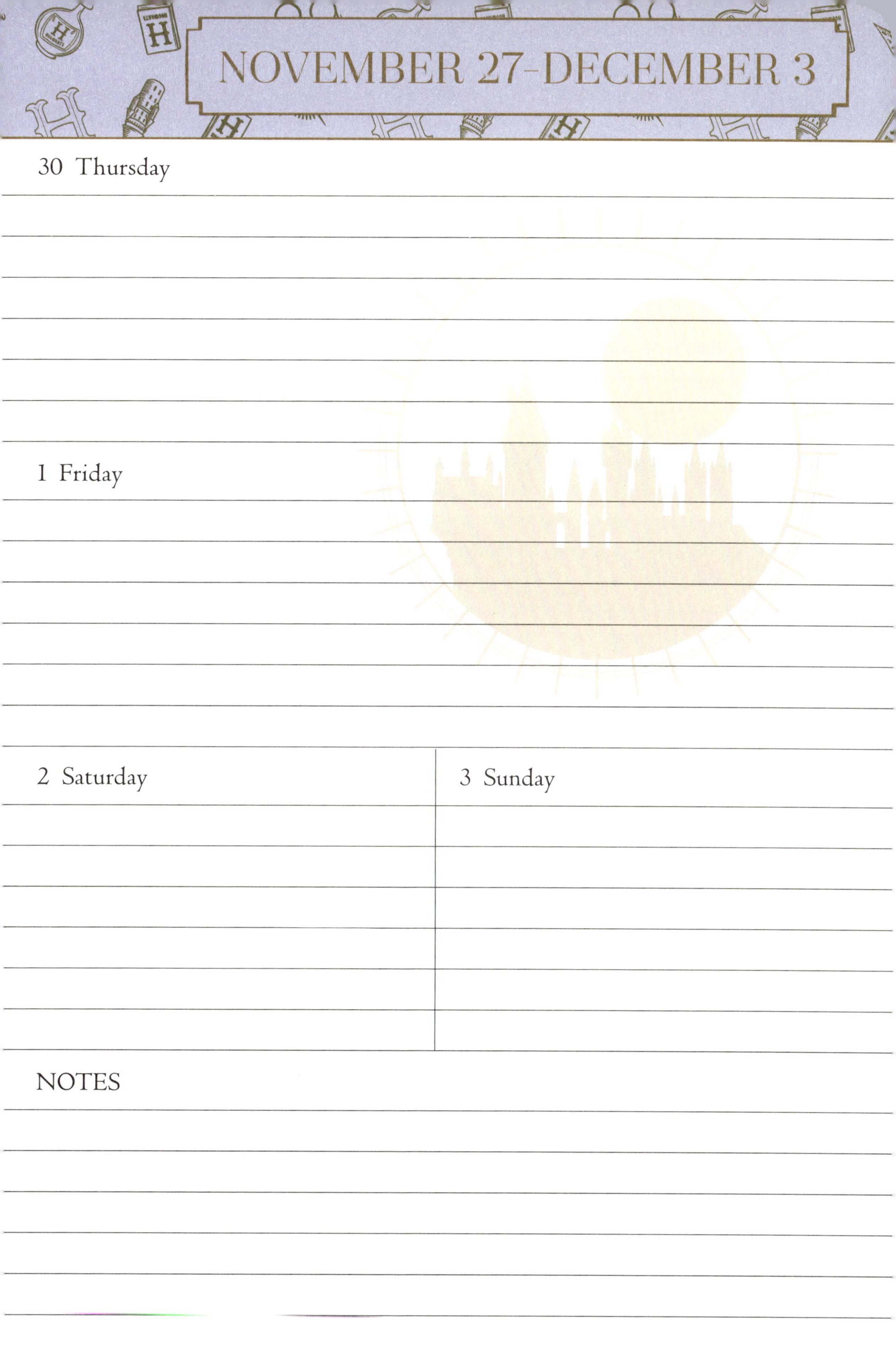

30 Thursday

1 Friday

2 Saturday

3 Sunday

NOTES

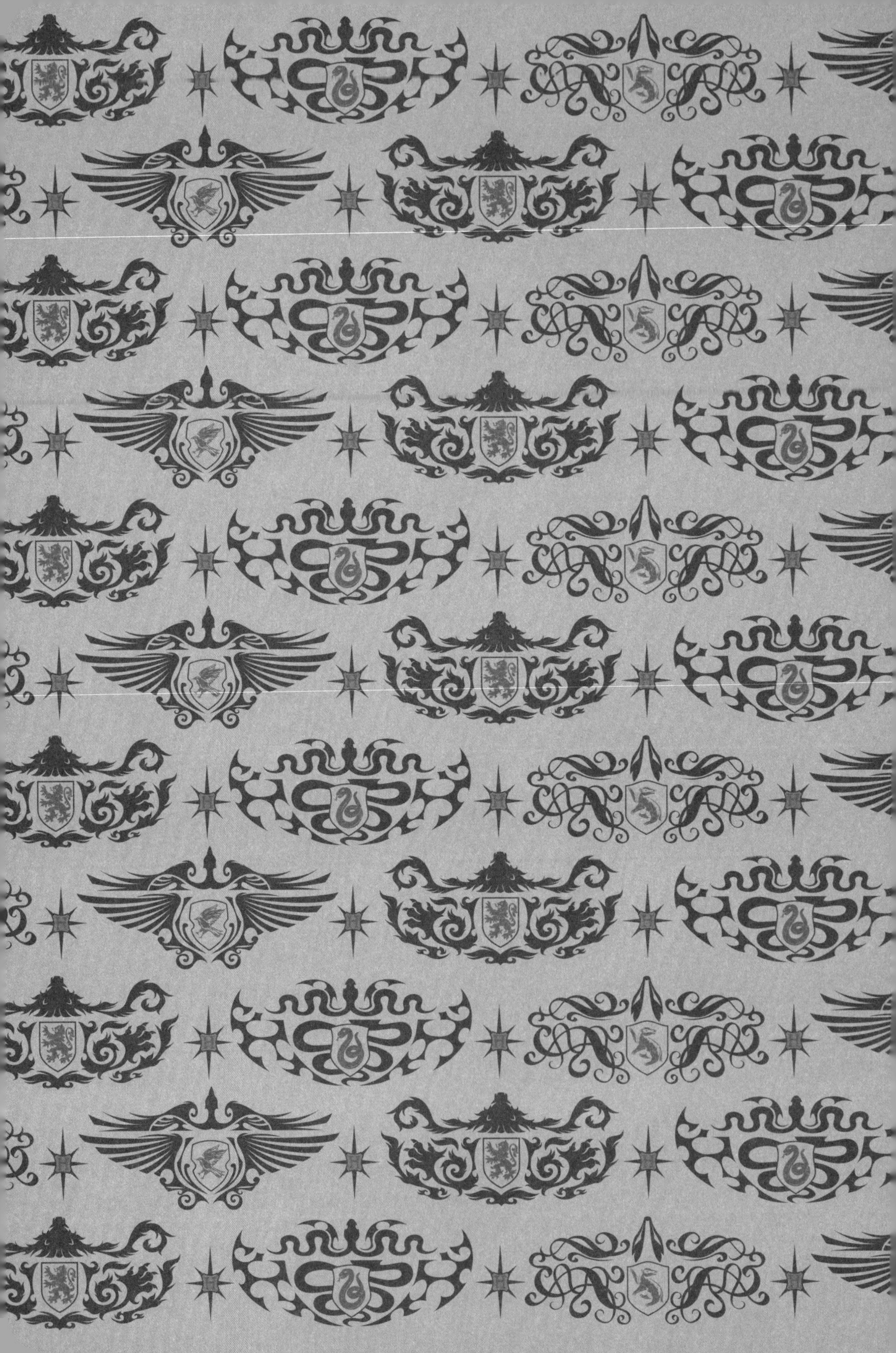

DEC

DECEMBER 2023

SUNDAY	MONDAY	TUESDAY	WEDNESDAY
3	4	5	6
10	11	12	13
17	18	19	20
24 Christmas Day Eve	25	26 First Day of Kwanzaa Boxing Day (UK)	27
31 New Year's Eve		Christmas Day	

THURSDAY	FRIDAY	SATURDAY	Notes
	1	2	
7	8	9	
Hanukkah Begins at Sundown			
14	15	16	
21	22	23	
28	29	30	

4 Monday

5 Tuesday

6 Wednesday

NOTES

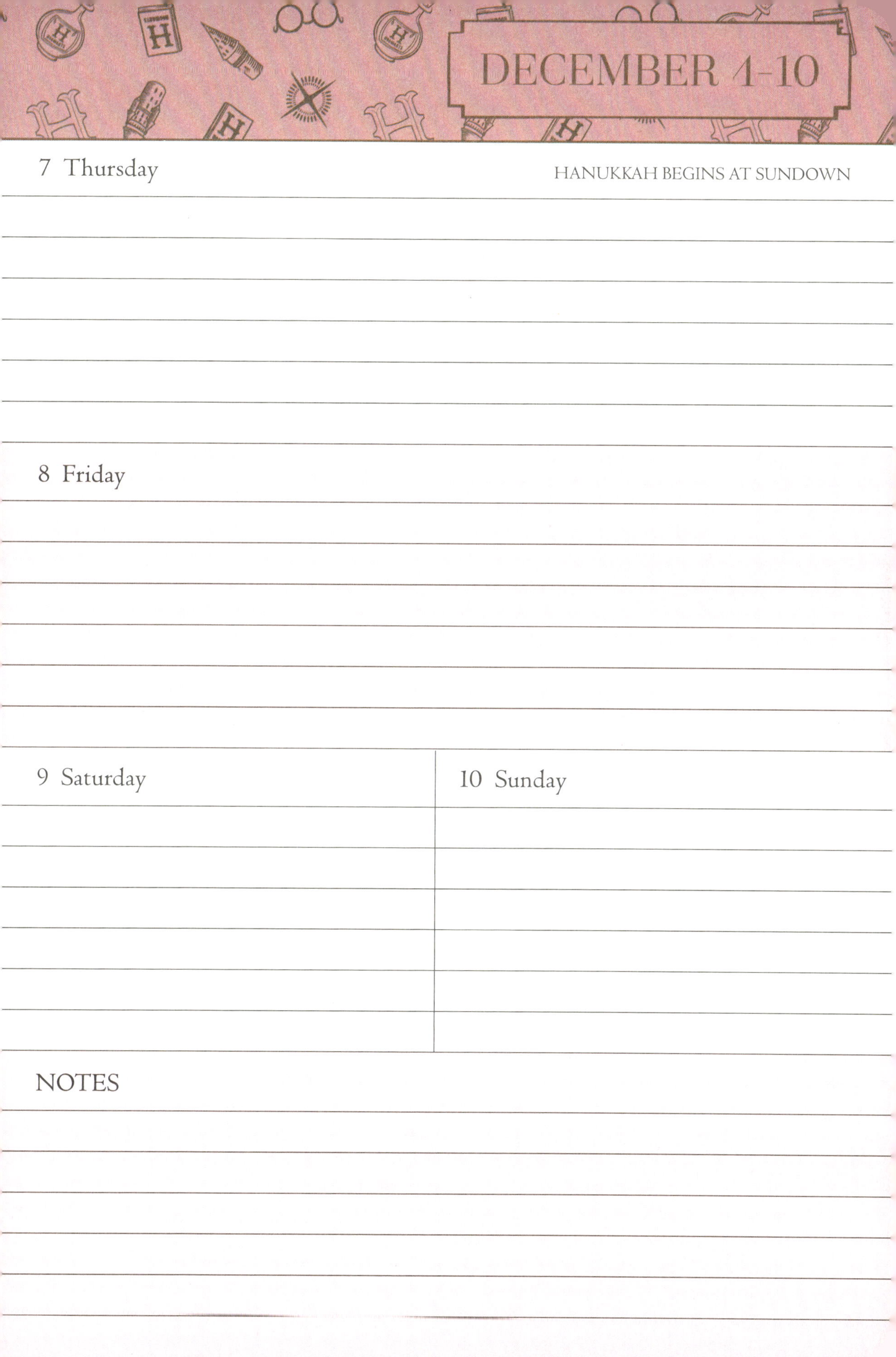

7 Thursday

HANUKKAH BEGINS AT SUNDOWN

8 Friday

9 Saturday

10 Sunday

NOTES

11 Monday

12 Tuesday

13 Wednesday

NOTES

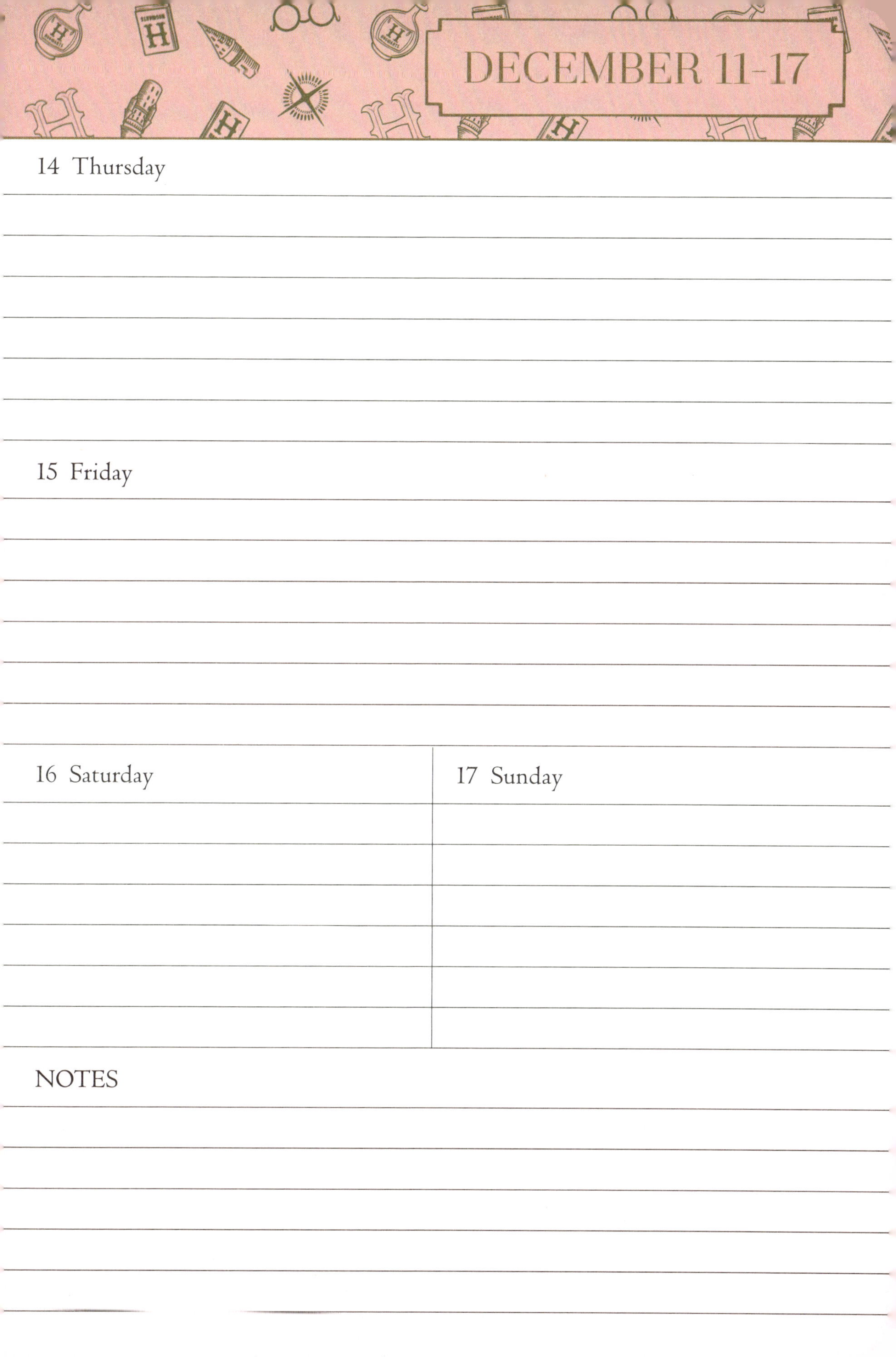

14 Thursday

15 Friday

16 Saturday

17 Sunday

NOTES

18 Monday

19 Tuesday

20 Wednesday

NOTES

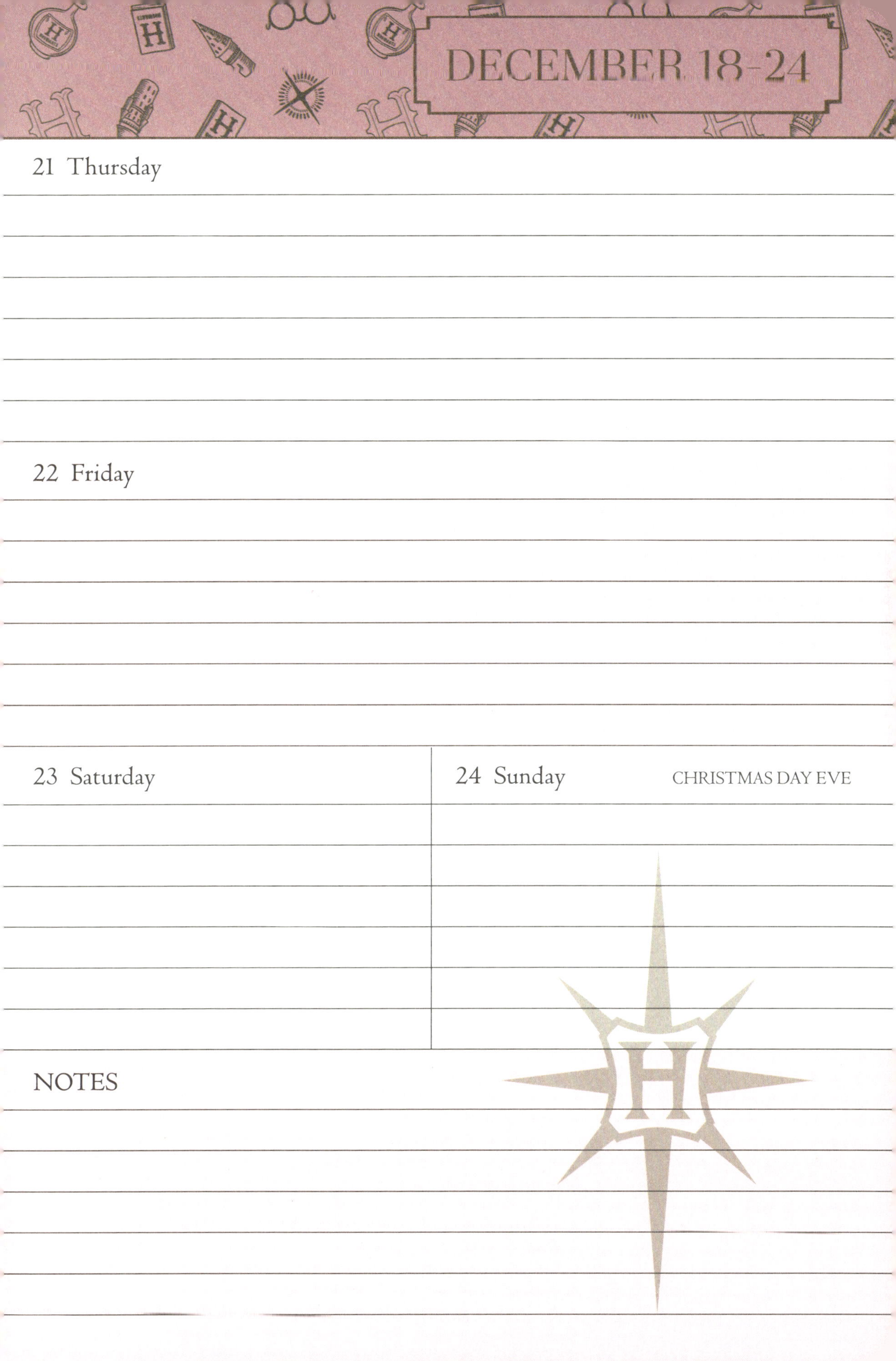

21 Thursday

22 Friday

23 Saturday

24 Sunday — CHRISTMAS DAY EVE

NOTES

DECEMBER 25–31

25 Monday

CHRISTMAS DAY

26 Tuesday

FIRST DAY OF KWANZAA
BOXING DAY (UK)

27 Wednesday

NOTES

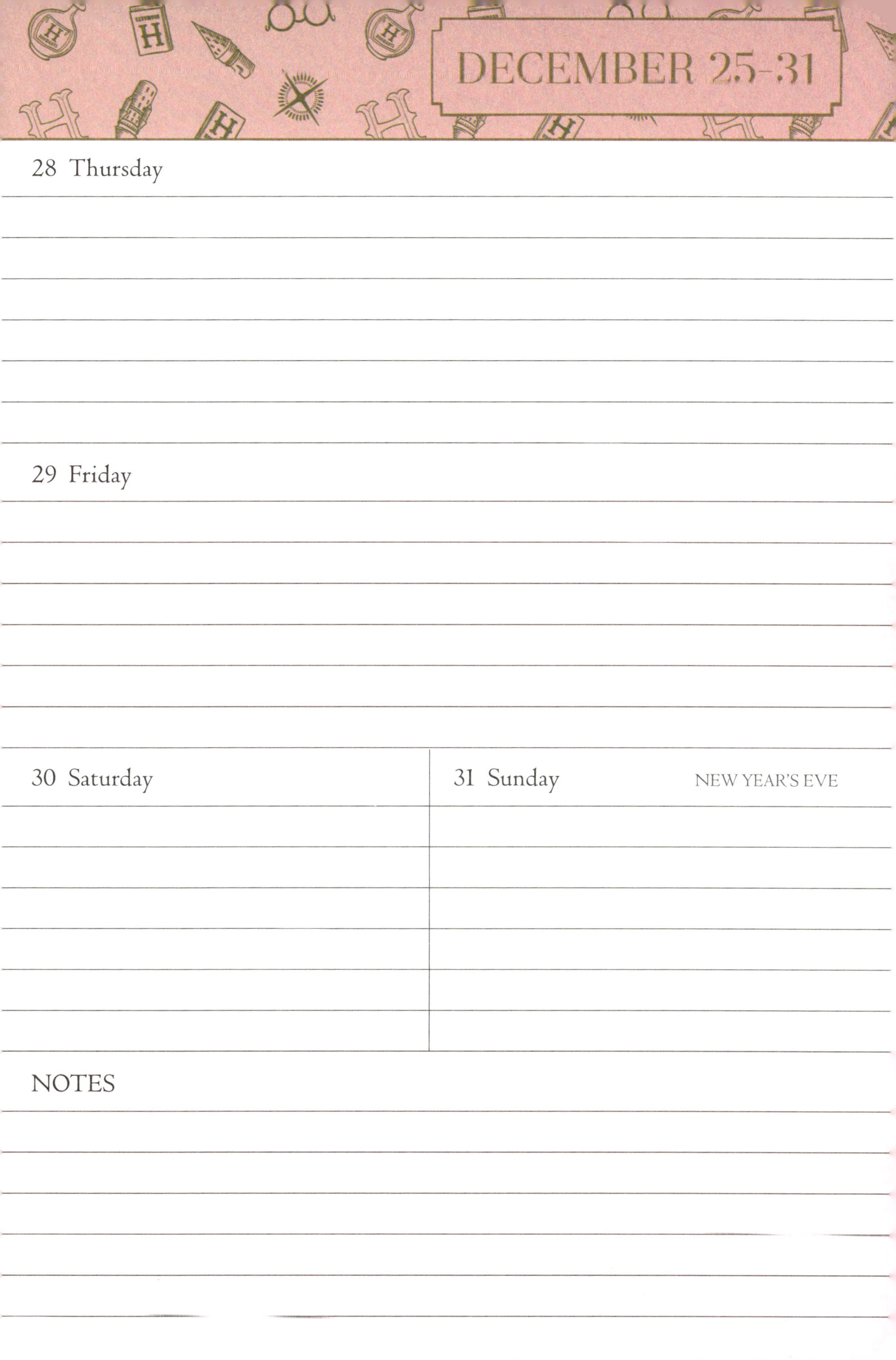

28 Thursday

29 Friday

30 Saturday

31 Sunday   NEW YEAR'S EVE

NOTES

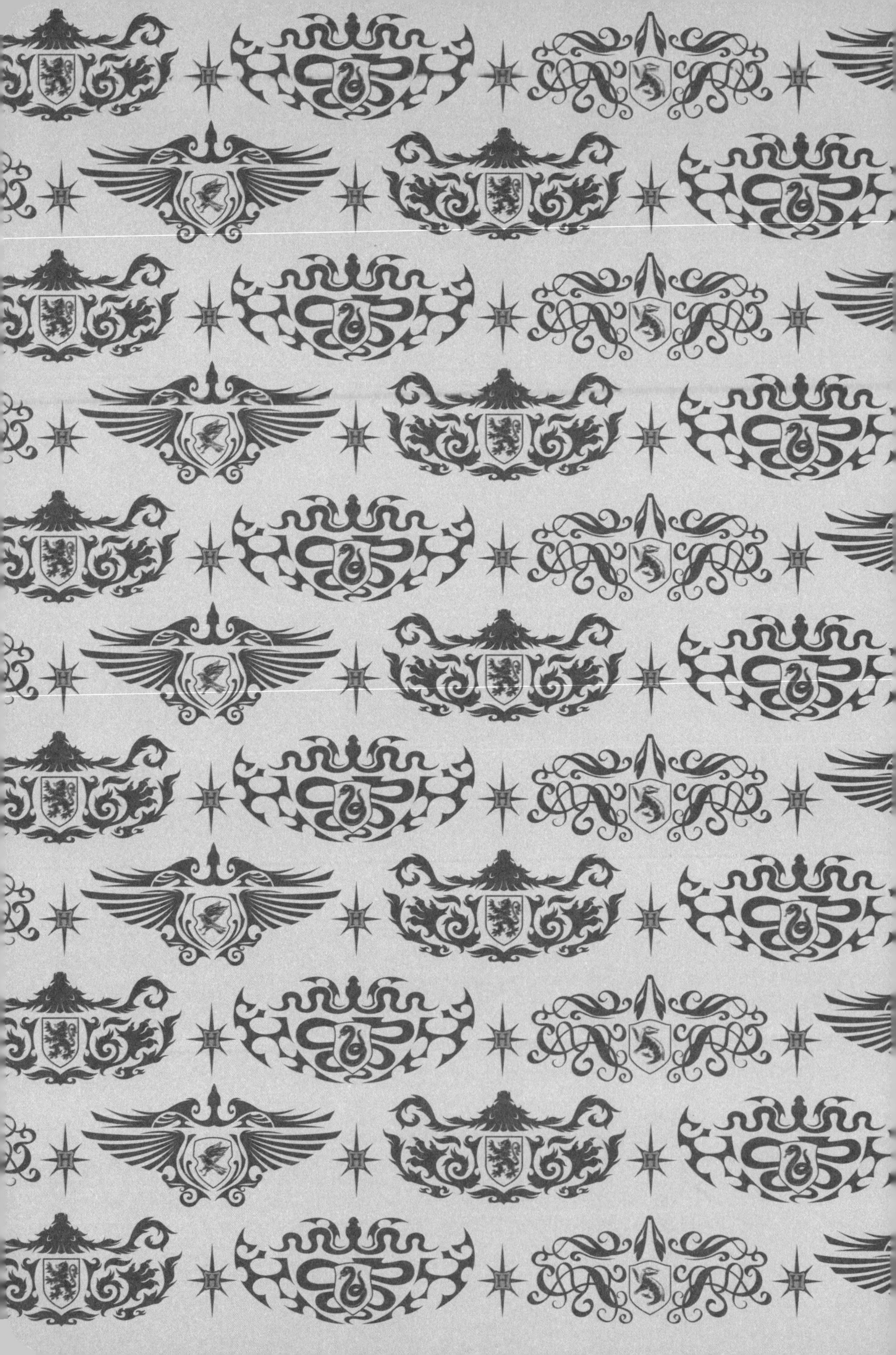

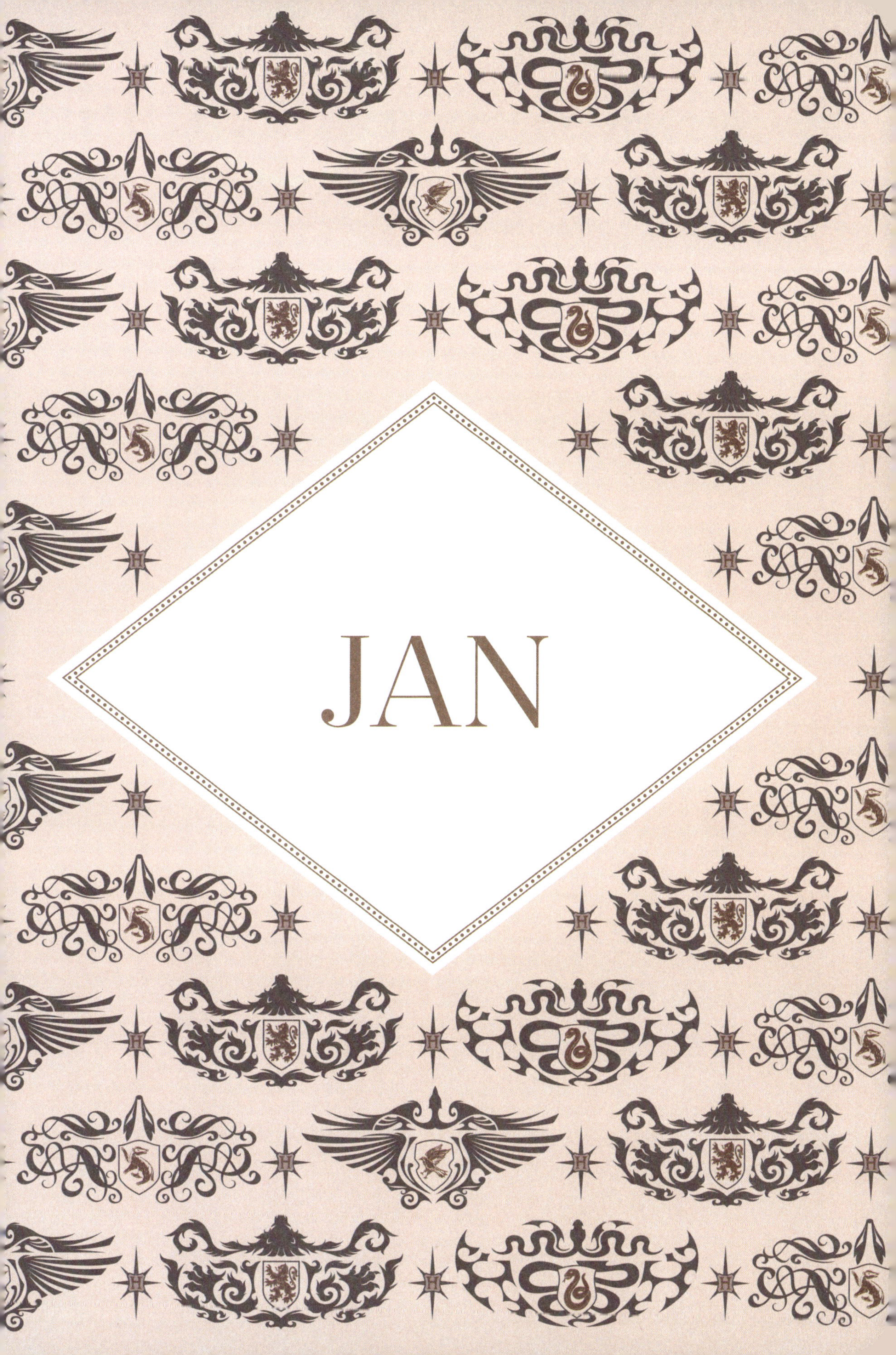
JAN

JANUARY 2024

SUNDAY	MONDAY	TUESDAY	WEDNESDAY
	1 New Year's Day	2	3
7	8	9	10
14	15 Martin Luther King Jr. Day	16	17
21	22	23	24
28	29	30	31

THURSDAY	FRIDAY	SATURDAY	Notes
4	5	6	
11	12	13	
18	19	20	
25	26	27	

1 Monday   NEW YEAR'S DAY

2 Tuesday

3 Wednesday

NOTES

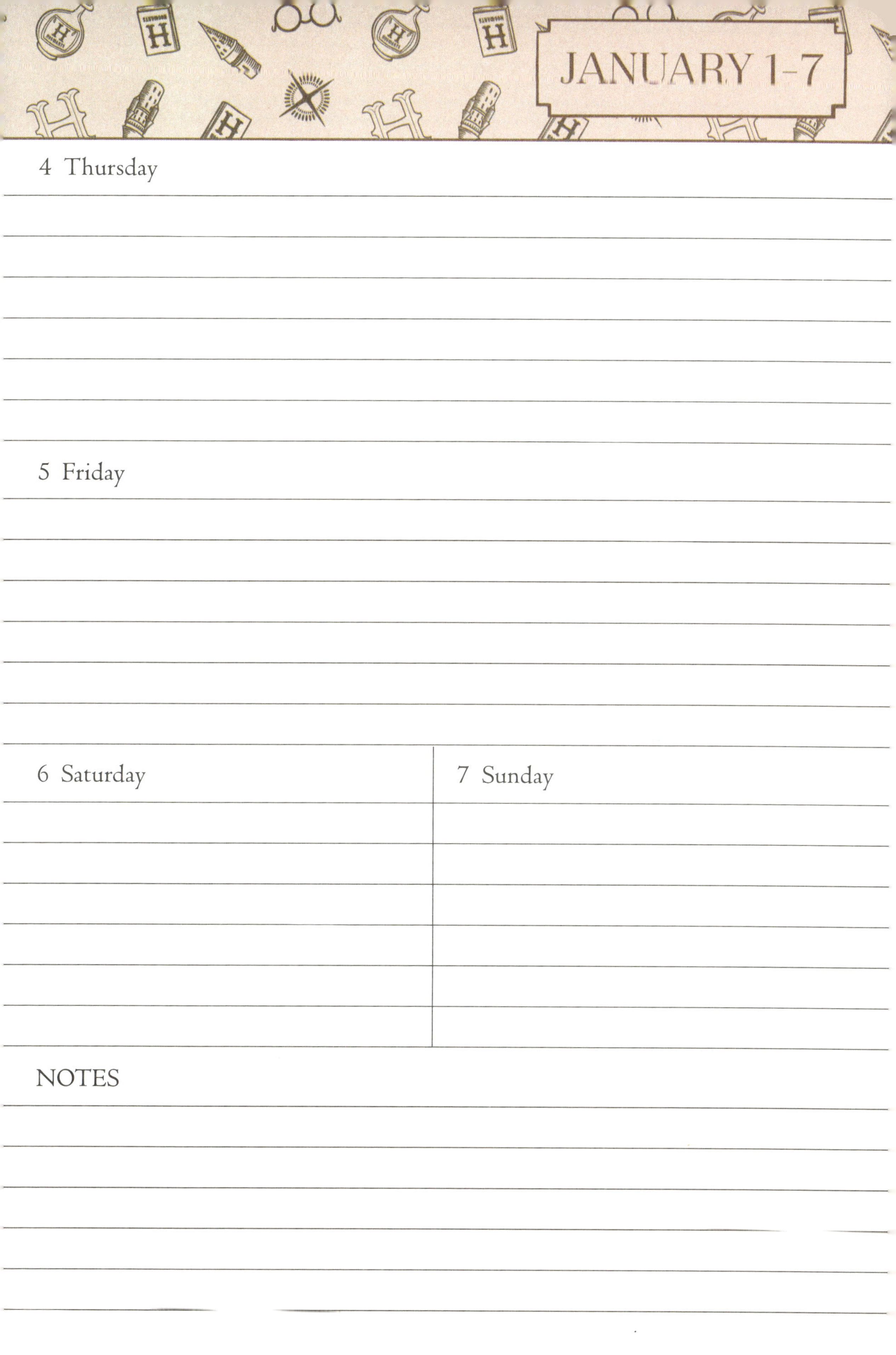

4 Thursday

5 Friday

6 Saturday

7 Sunday

NOTES

8 Monday

9 Tuesday

10 Wednesday

NOTES

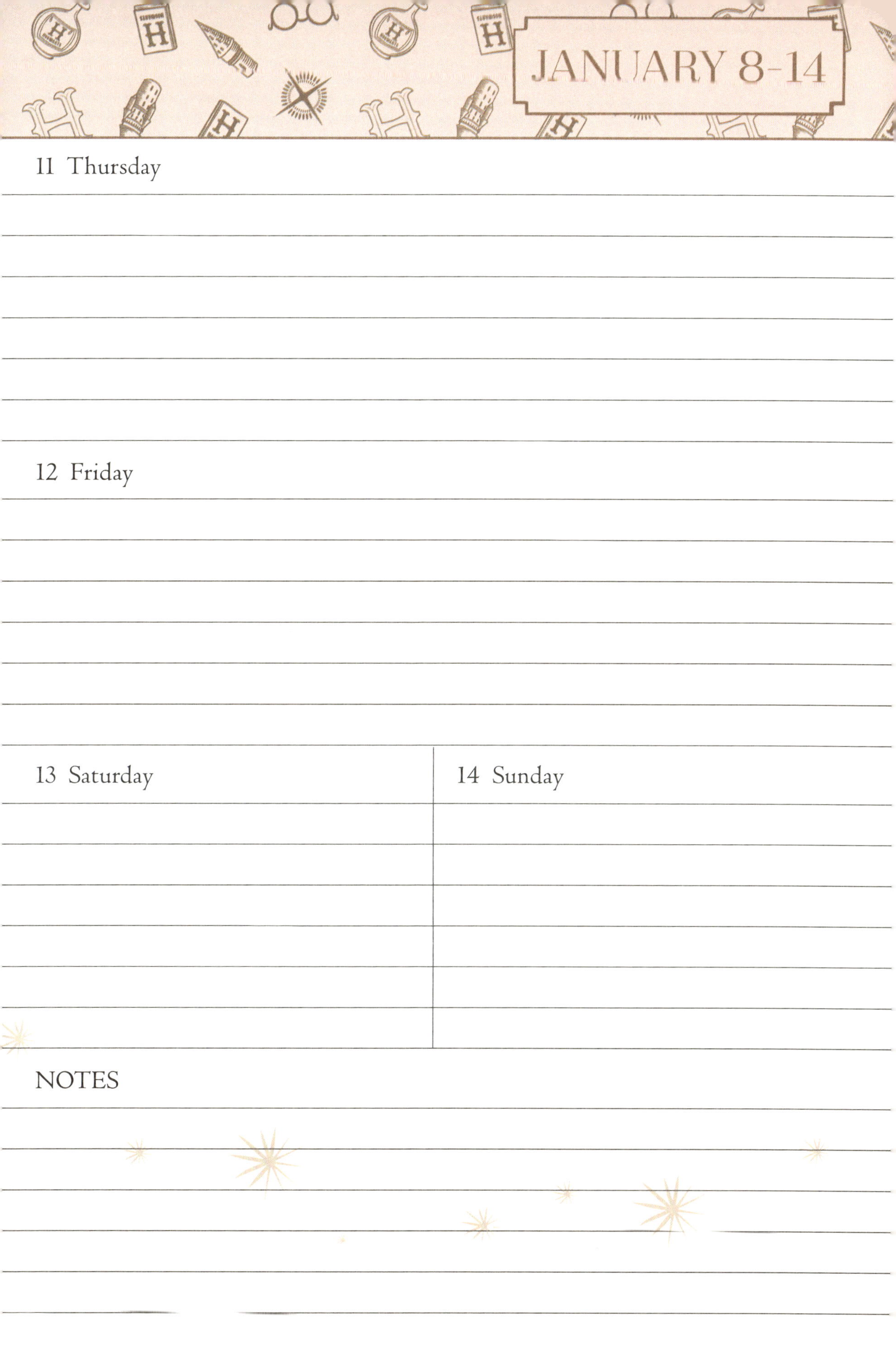

11 Thursday

12 Friday

13 Saturday

14 Sunday

NOTES

15 Monday   MARTIN LUTHER KING JR. DAY

16 Tuesday

17 Wednesday

NOTES

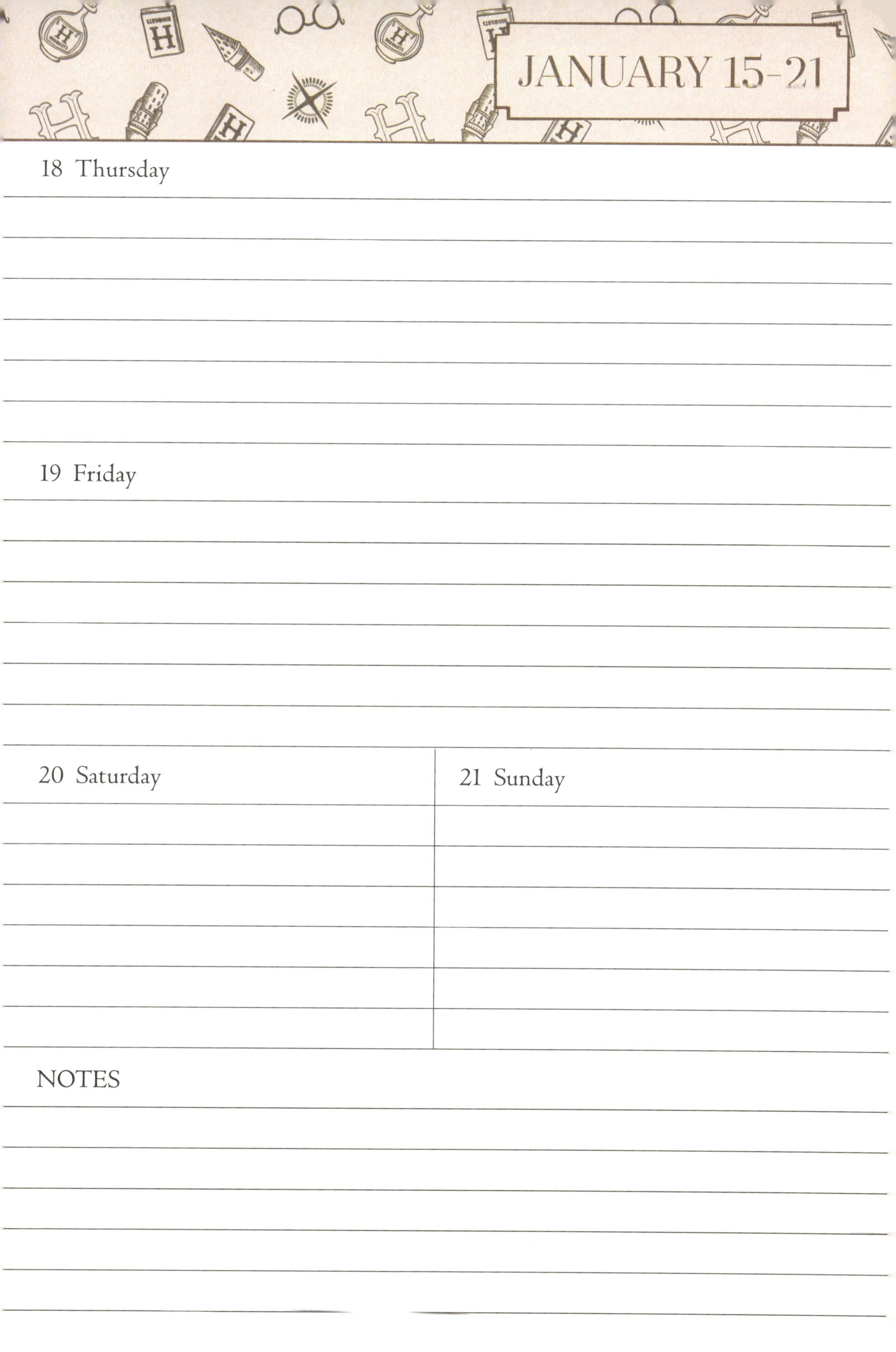

18 Thursday

19 Friday

20 Saturday

21 Sunday

NOTES

22 Monday

23 Tuesday

24 Wednesday

NOTES

25 Thursday

26 Friday

27 Saturday

28 Sunday

NOTES

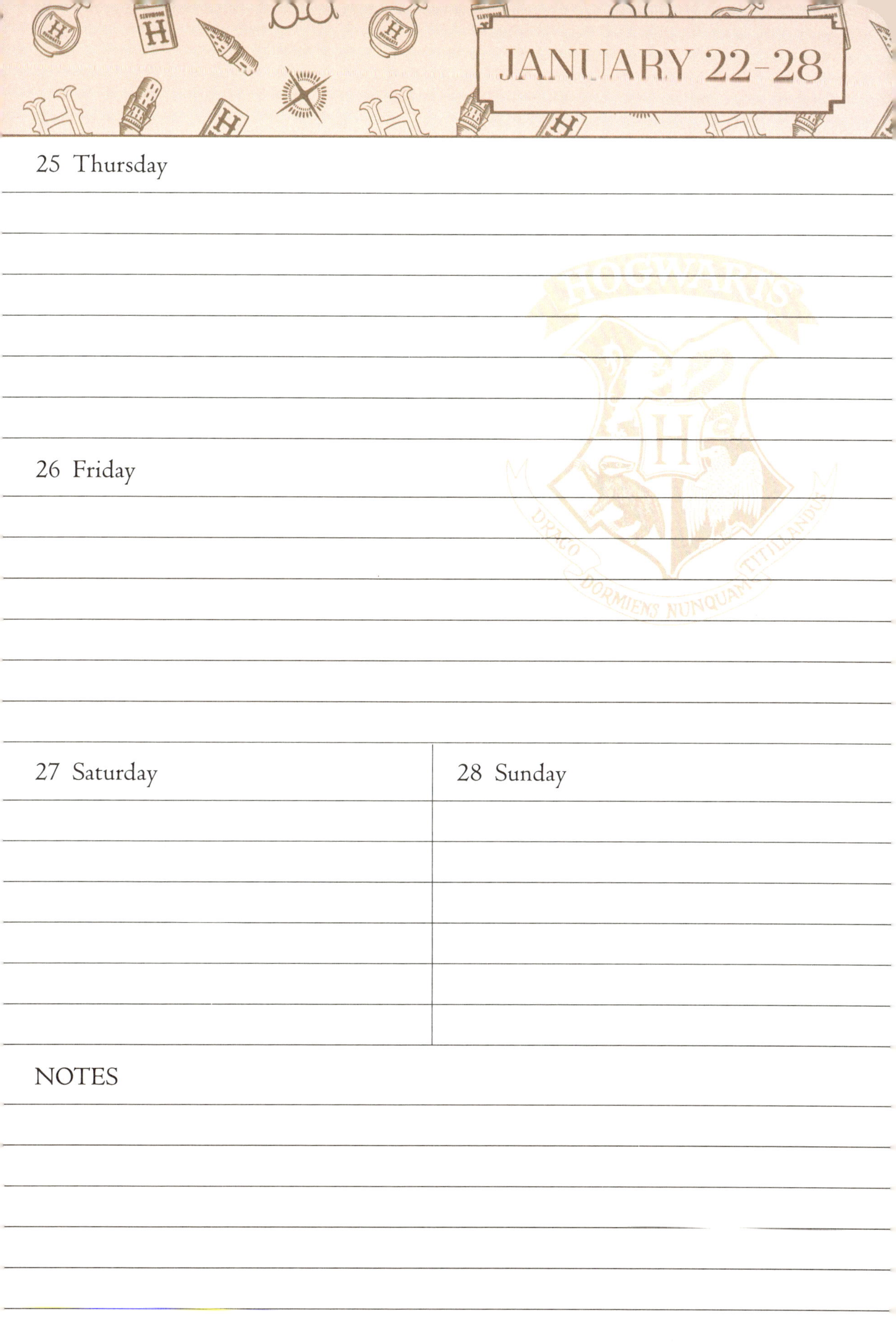

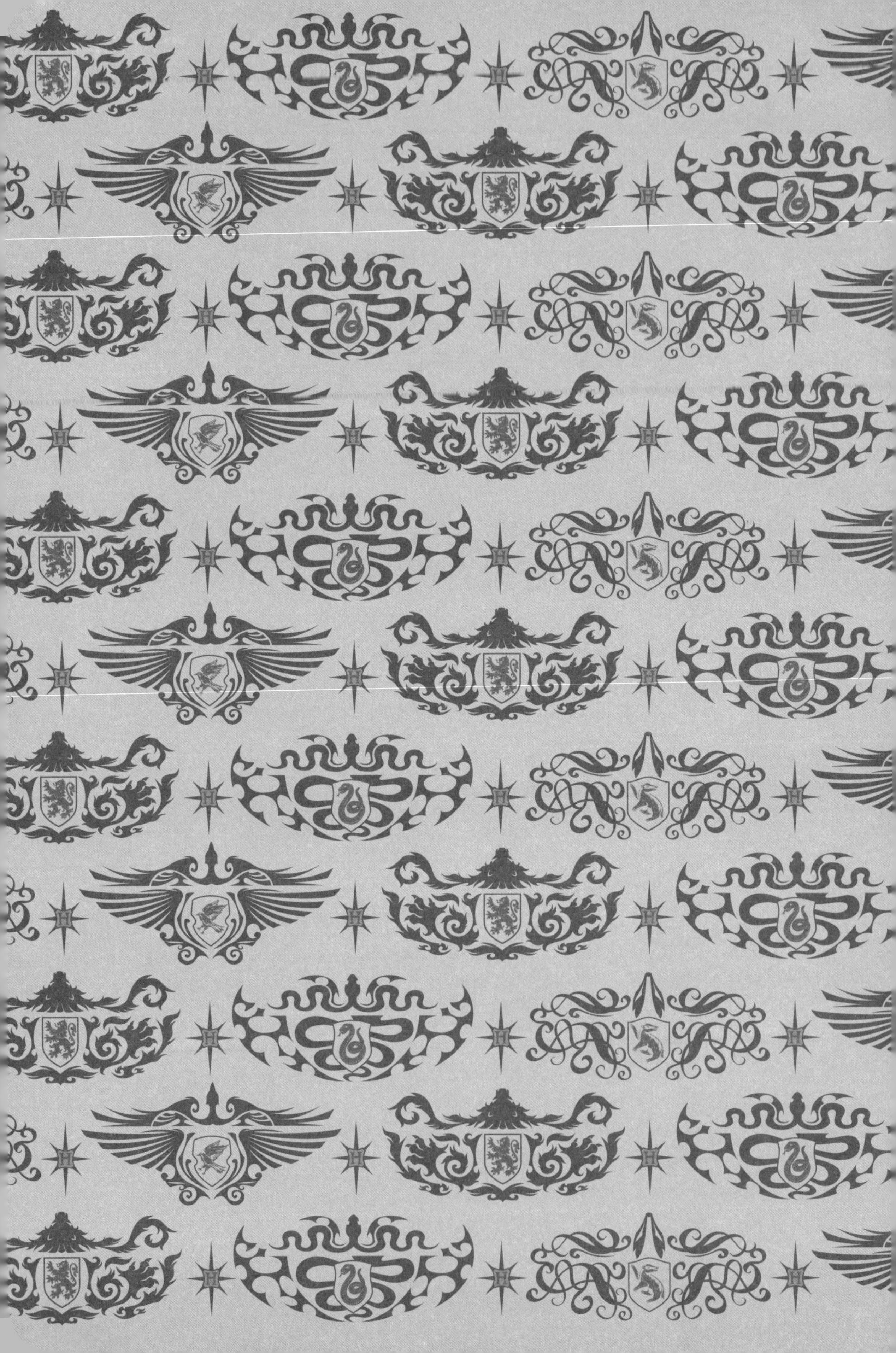

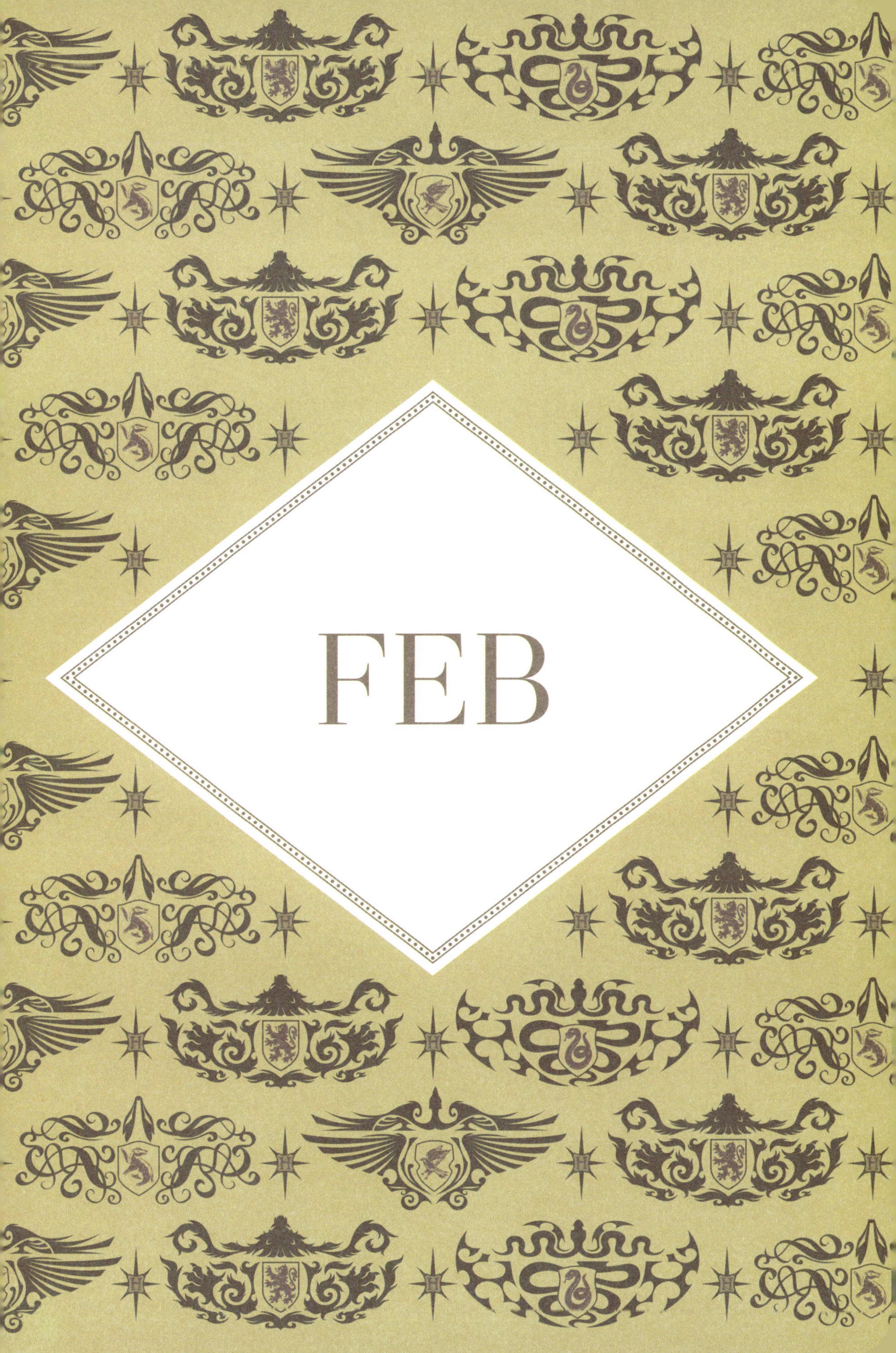

FEB

FEBRUARY 2024

SUNDAY	MONDAY	TUESDAY	WEDNESDAY
4	5	6	7
11	12	13	14 Valentine's Day
18	19 Presidents' Day	20	21
25	26	27	28

FEBRUARY 2024

THURSDAY	FRIDAY	SATURDAY	Notes
1	2 Groundhog Day	3	
8	9	10	
15	16	17	
22	23	24	
29			

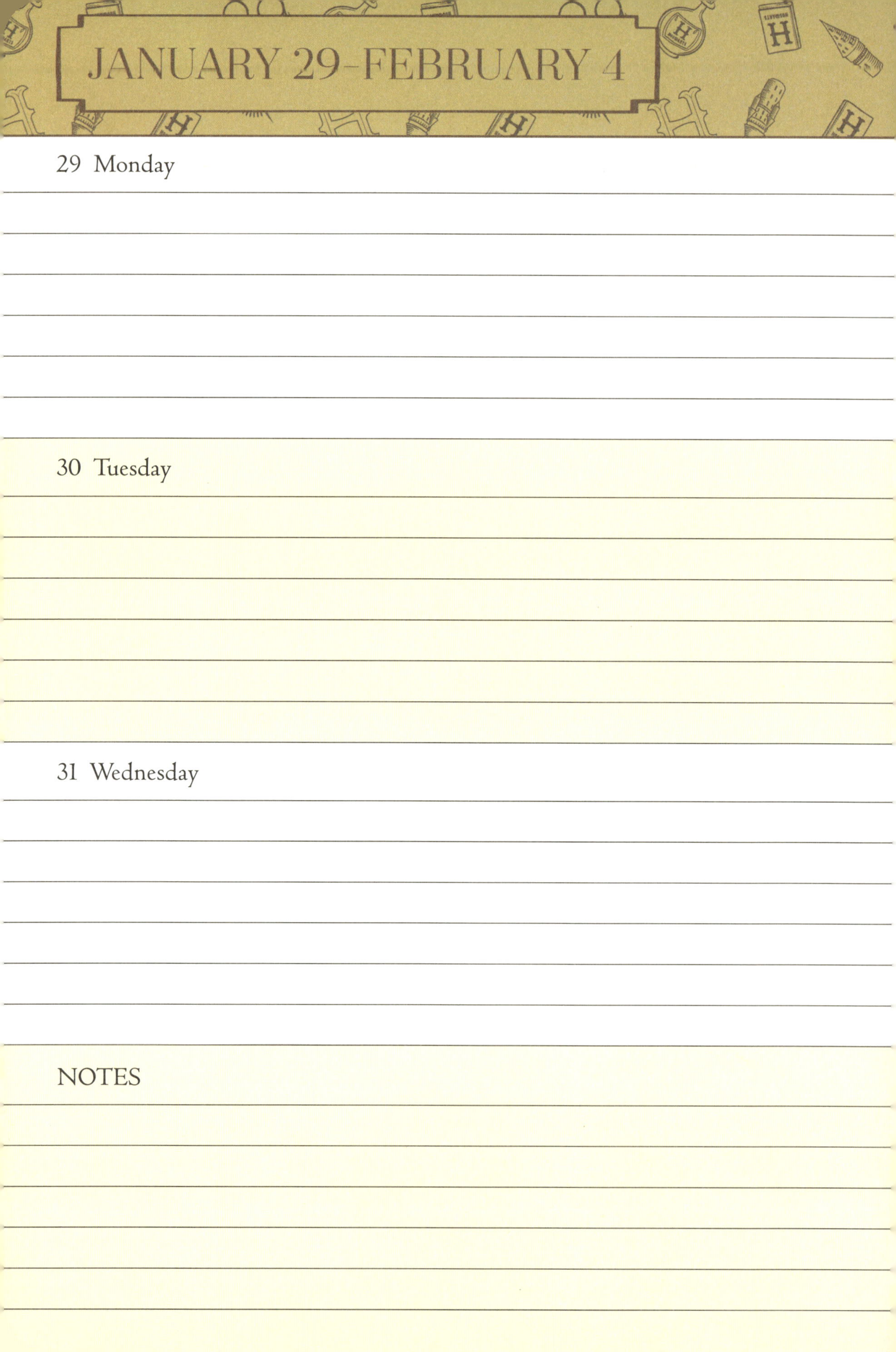

29 Monday

30 Tuesday

31 Wednesday

NOTES

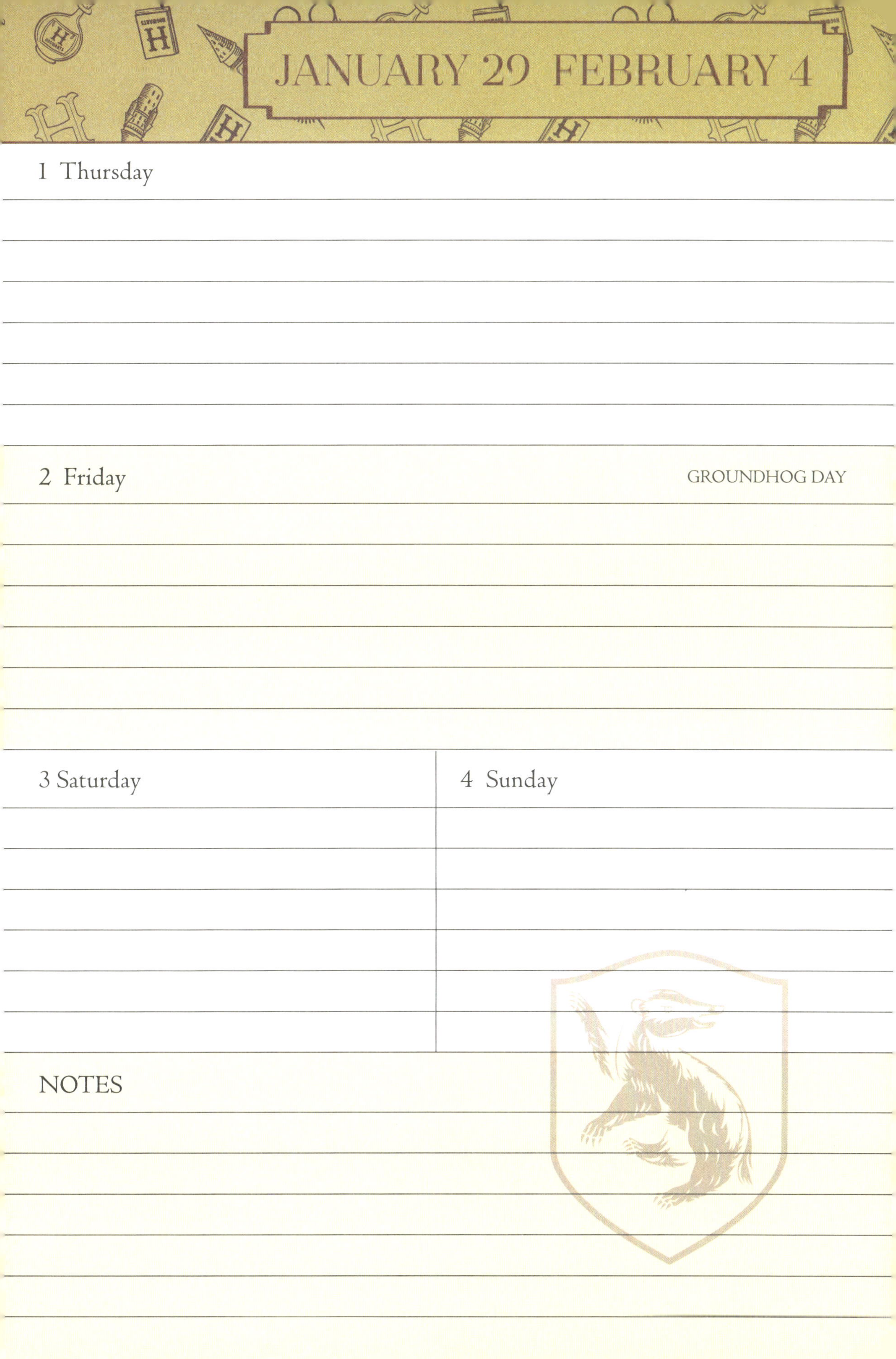

JANUARY 29 FEBRUARY 4

1 Thursday

2 Friday   GROUNDHOG DAY

3 Saturday   **4 Sunday**

NOTES

5 Monday

6 Tuesday

7 Wednesday

NOTES

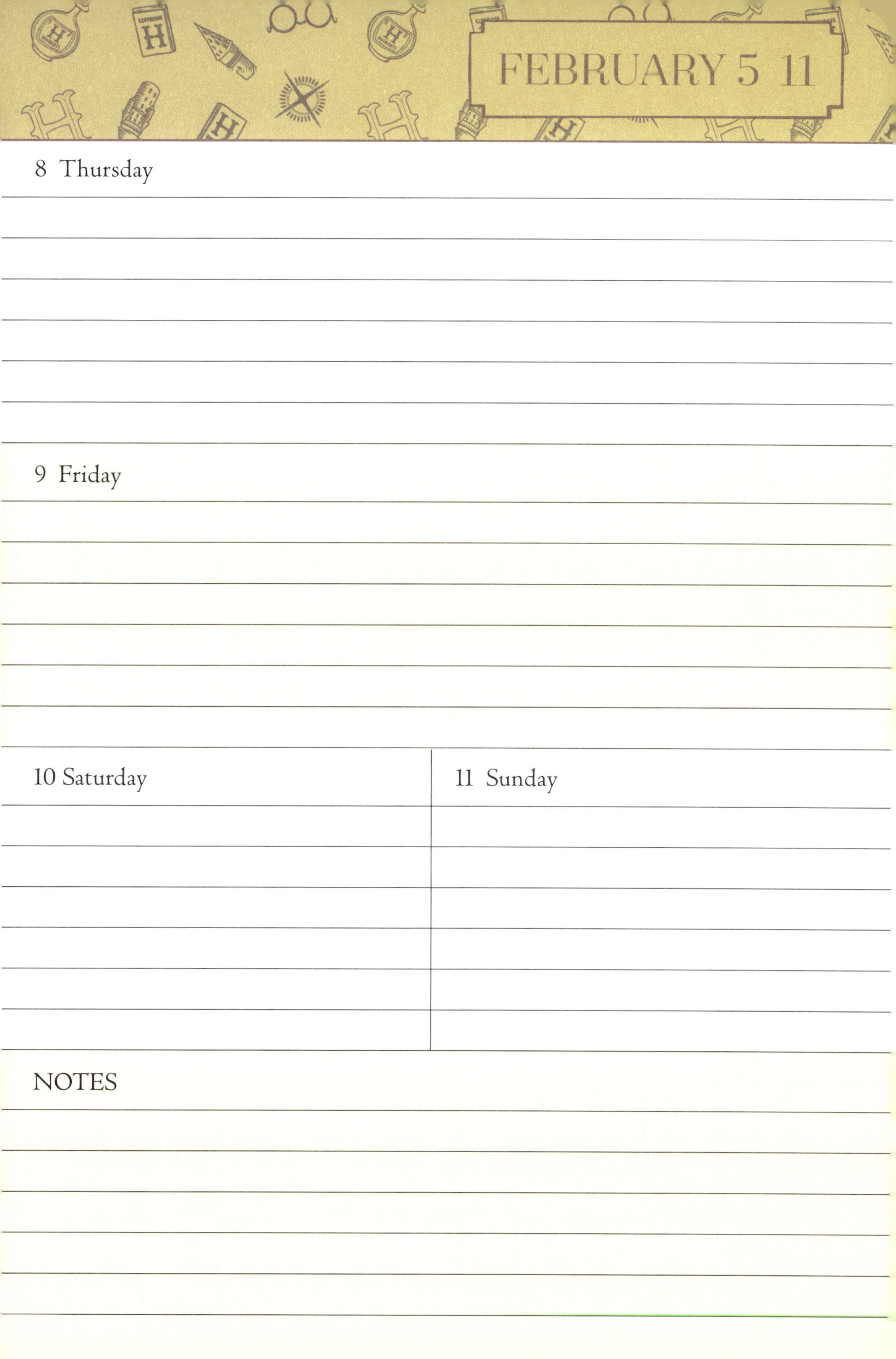

8 Thursday

9 Friday

10 Saturday

11 Sunday

NOTES

12 Monday

13 Tuesday

14 Wednesday

VALENTINE'S DAY

NOTES

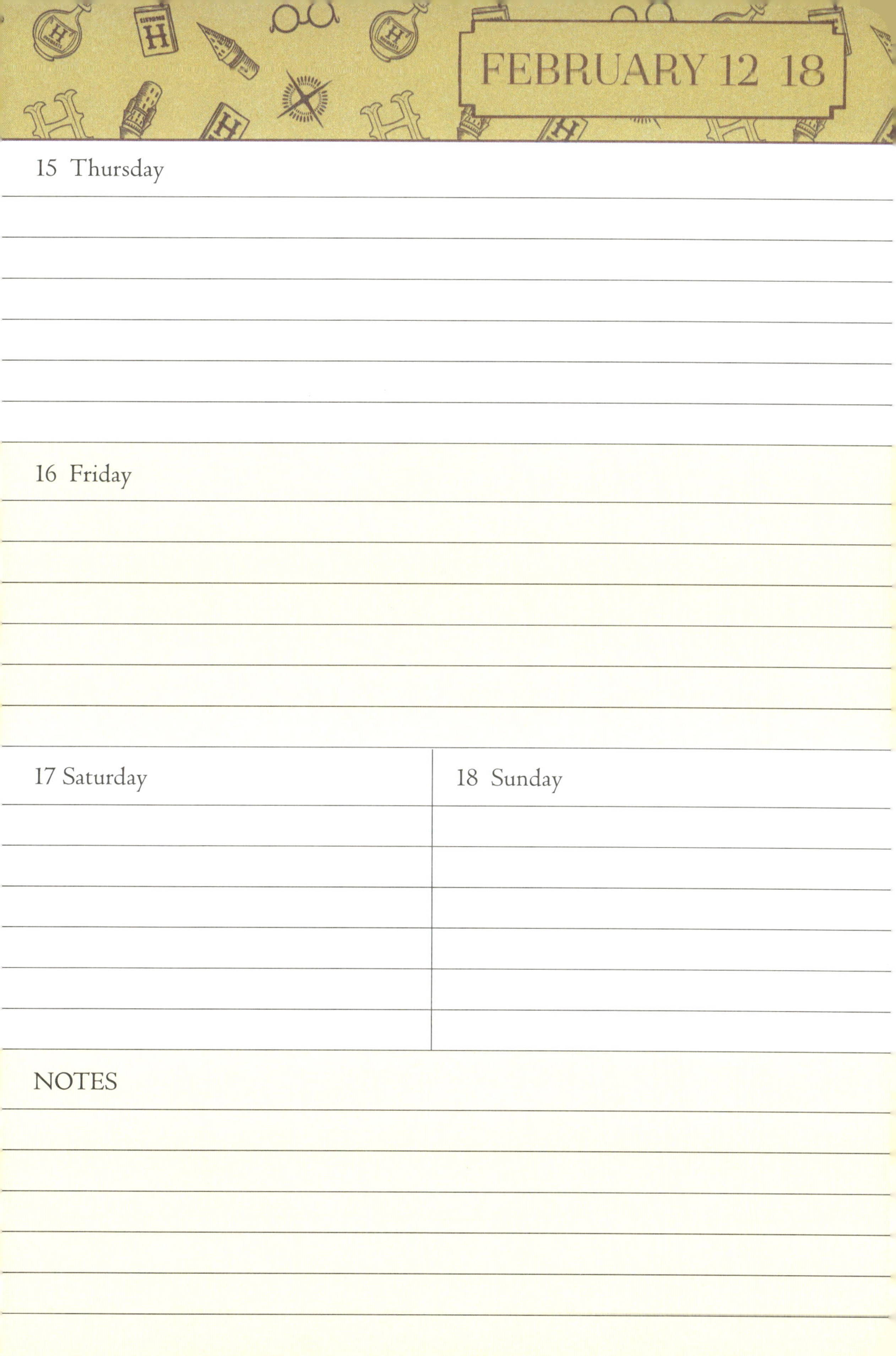

15 Thursday

16 Friday

17 Saturday

18 Sunday

NOTES

19 Monday   PRESIDENTS' DAY

20 Tuesday

21 Wednesday

NOTES

22 Thursday

23 Friday

24 Saturday

25 Sunday

NOTES

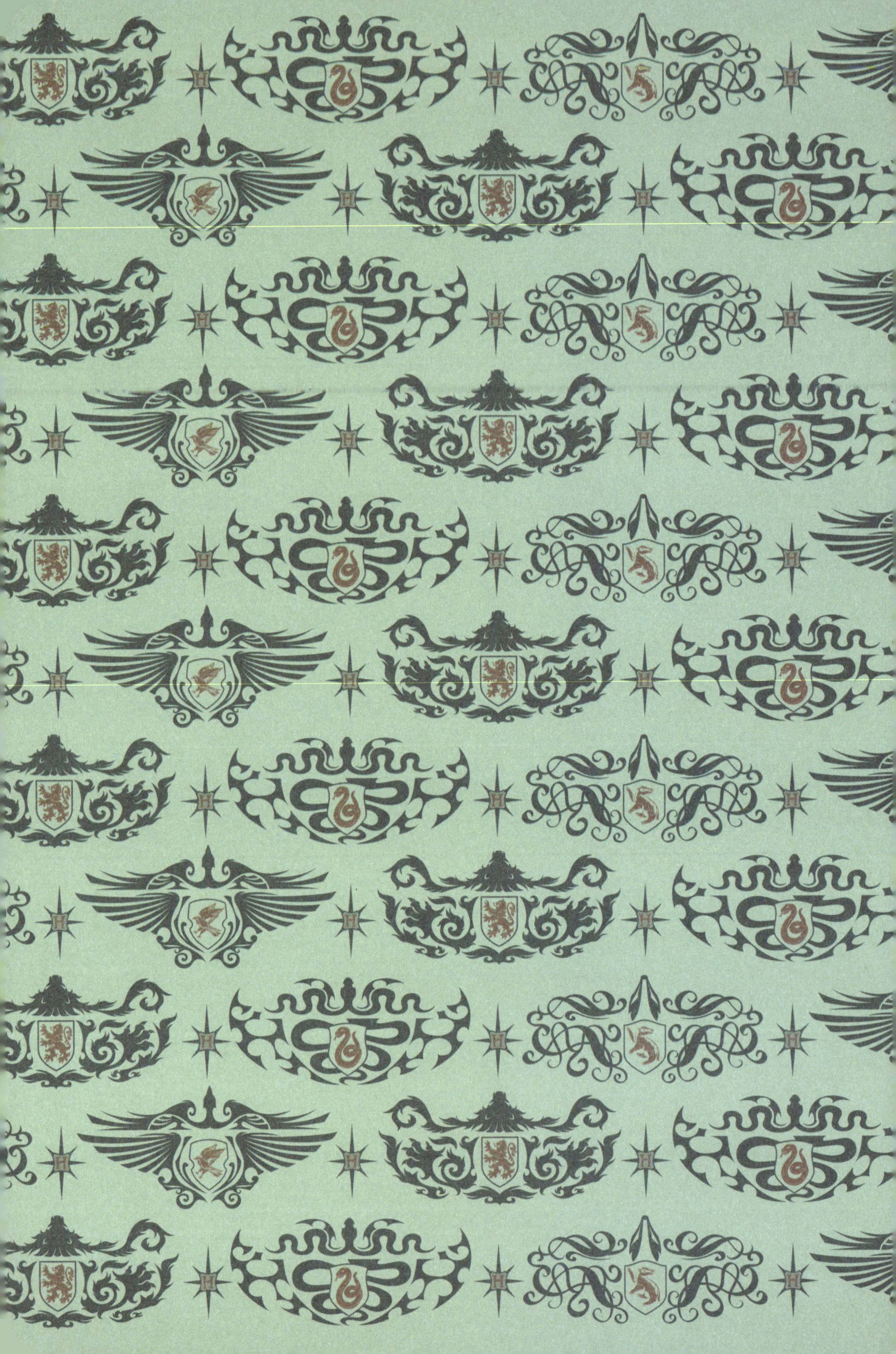

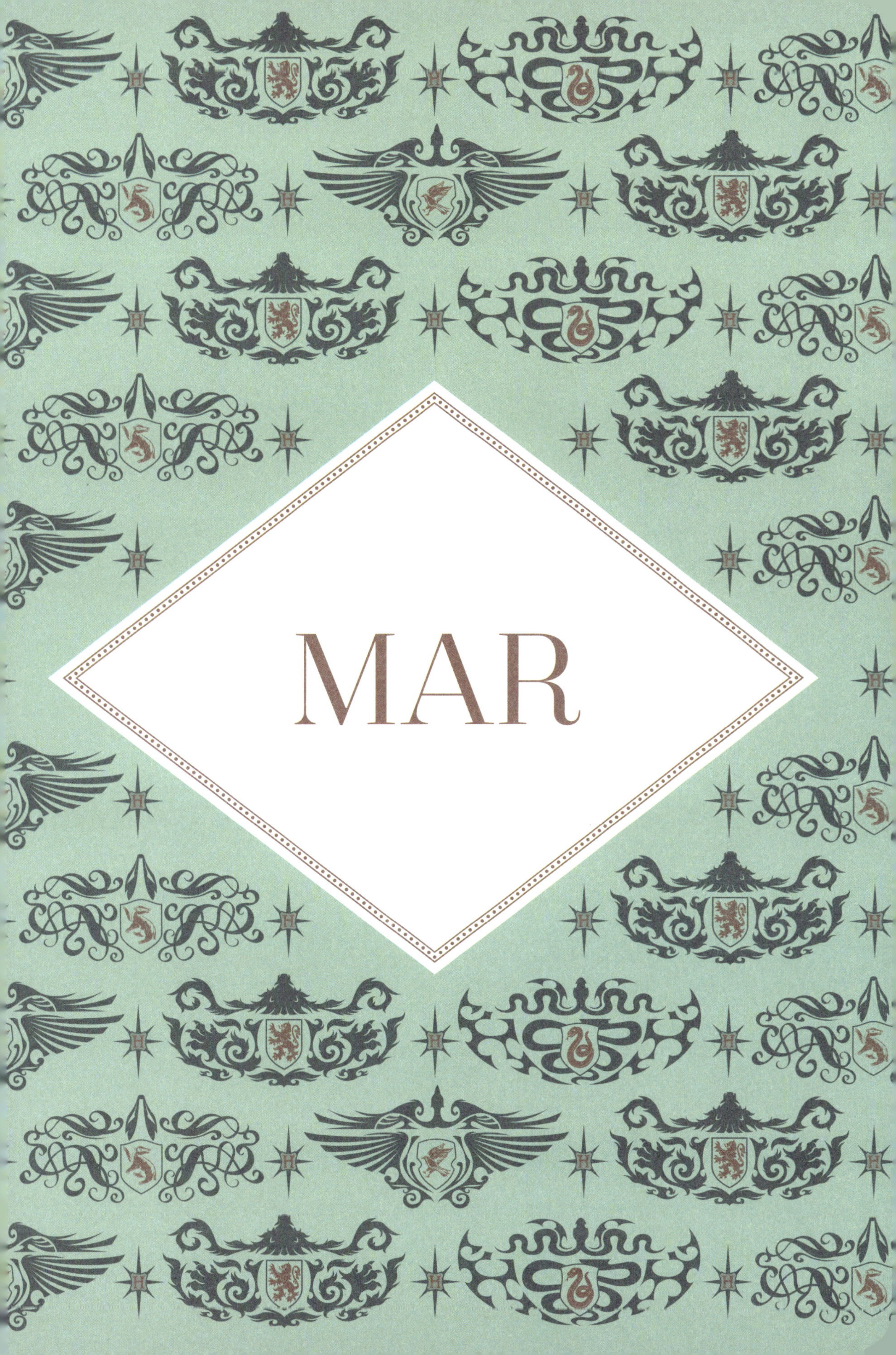
MAR

MARCH 2024

3	4	5	6
10	11	12	13
Daylight Savings Time Begins			
17	18	19	20
Saint Patrick's Day			
24	25	26	27
31			
Easter			

THURSDAY	FRIDAY	SATURDAY	Notes
	1 Ron Weasley's Birthday	2	
7	8	9	
14	15	16	
21	22	23	
28	29 Good Friday	30	

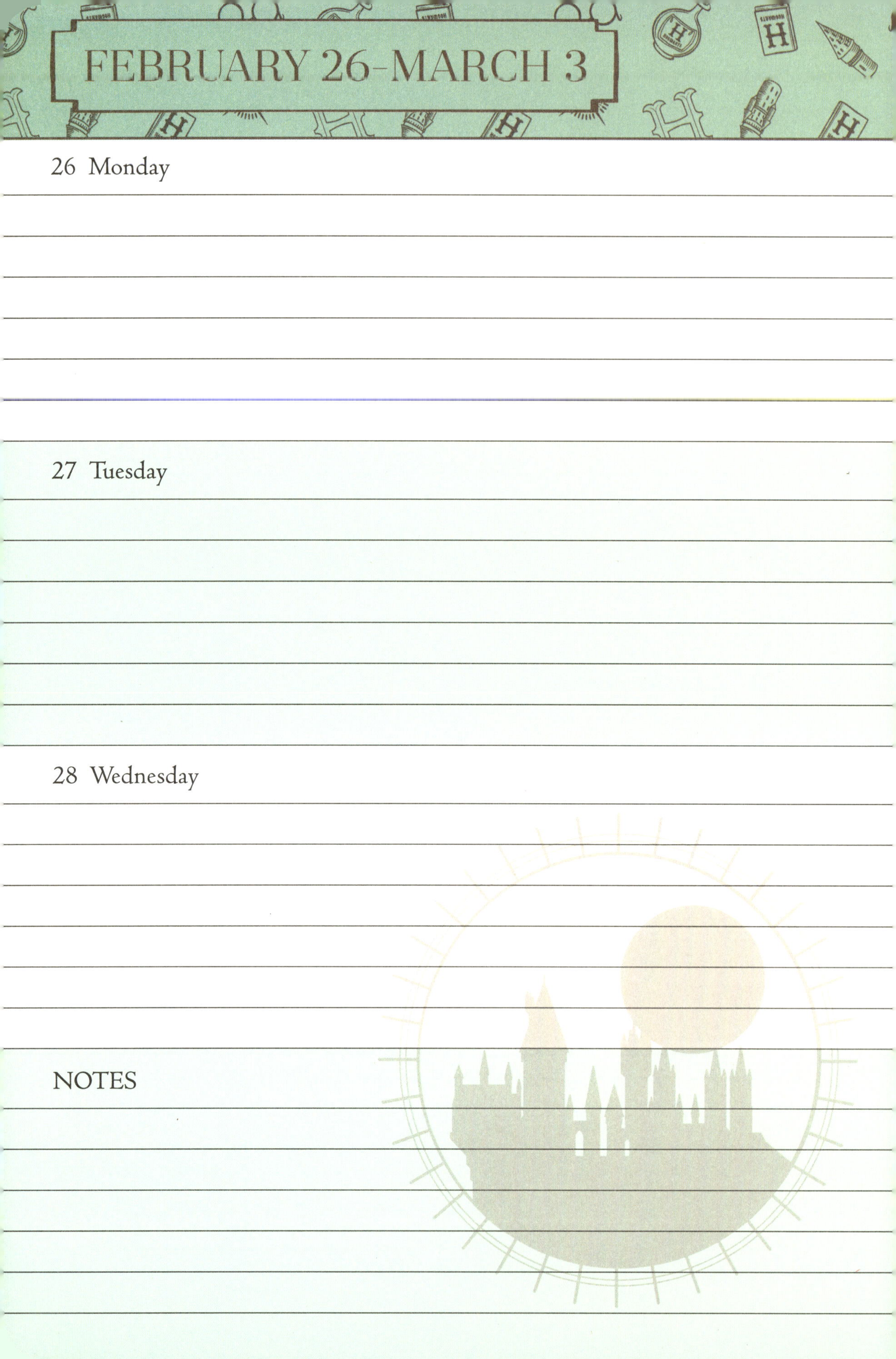

26 Monday

27 Tuesday

28 Wednesday

NOTES

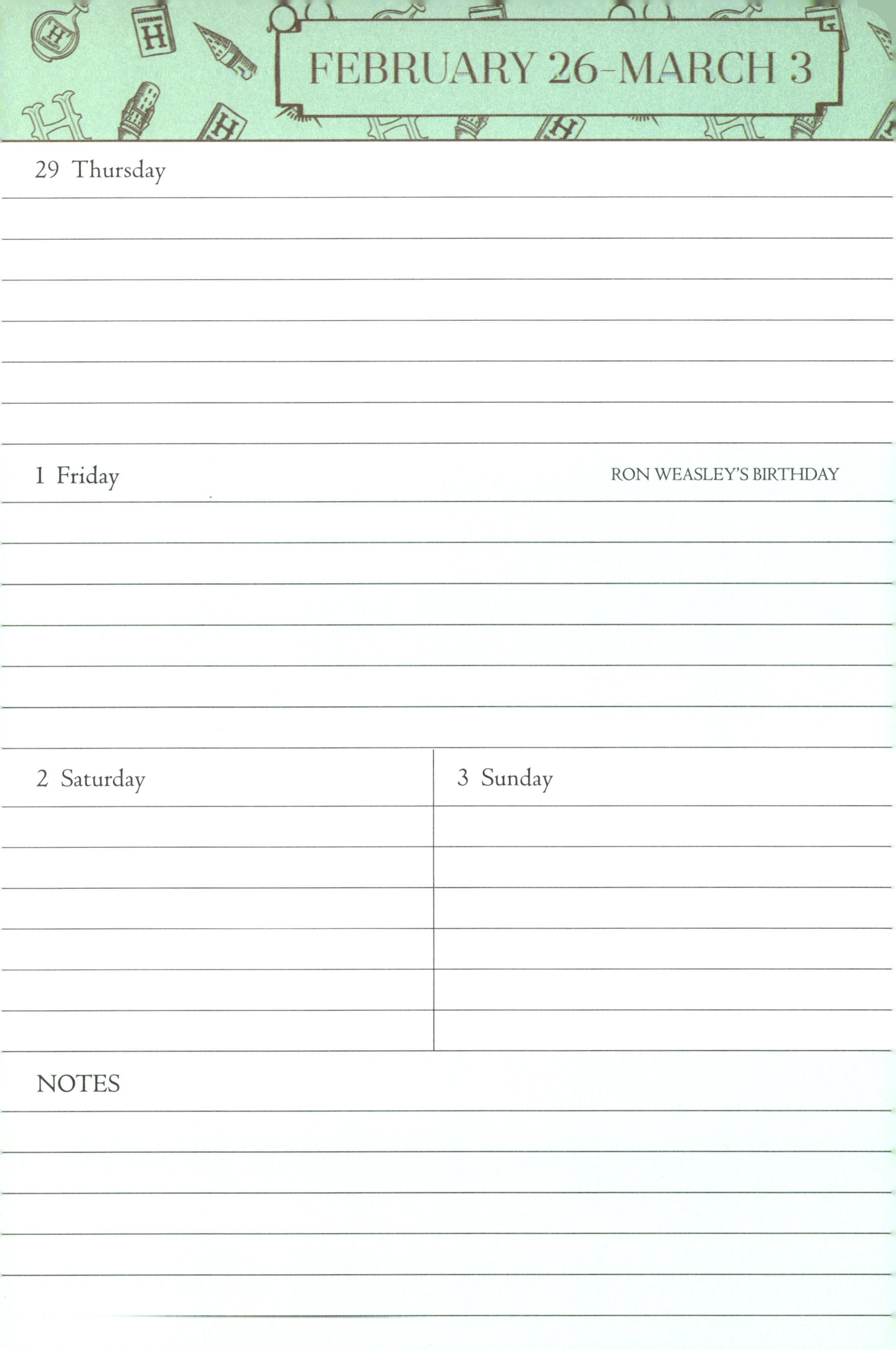

29 Thursday

1 Friday   RON WEASLEY'S BIRTHDAY

2 Saturday

3 Sunday

NOTES

4 Monday

5 Tuesday

6 Wednesday

NOTES

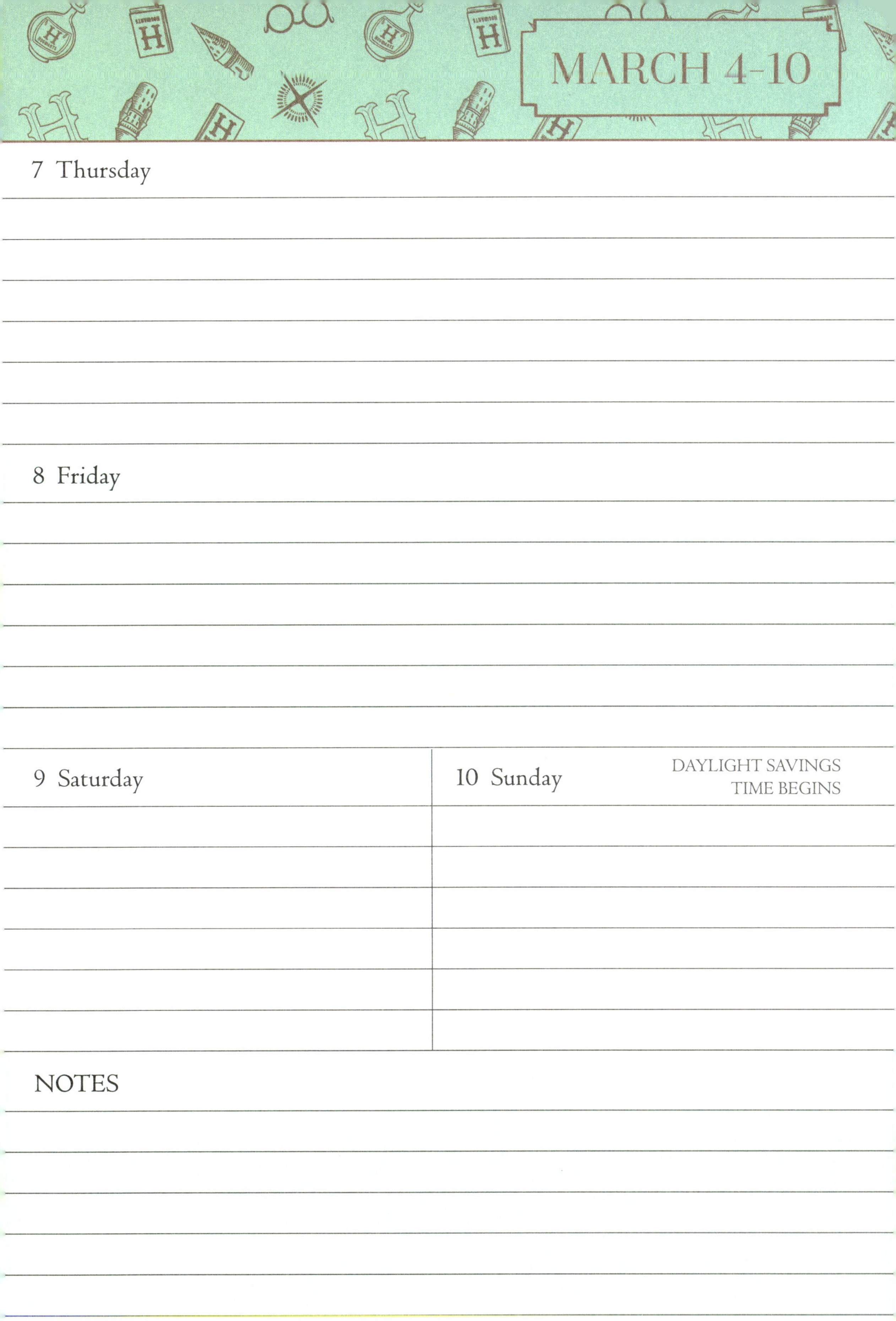

7 Thursday

8 Friday

9 Saturday

10 Sunday DAYLIGHT SAVINGS TIME BEGINS

NOTES

11 Monday

12 Tuesday

13 Wednesday

NOTES

14 Thursday

15 Friday

16 Saturday

17 Sunday   SAINT PATRICK'S DAY

NOTES

MARCH 18-24

18 Monday

19 Tuesday

20 Wednesday

NOTES

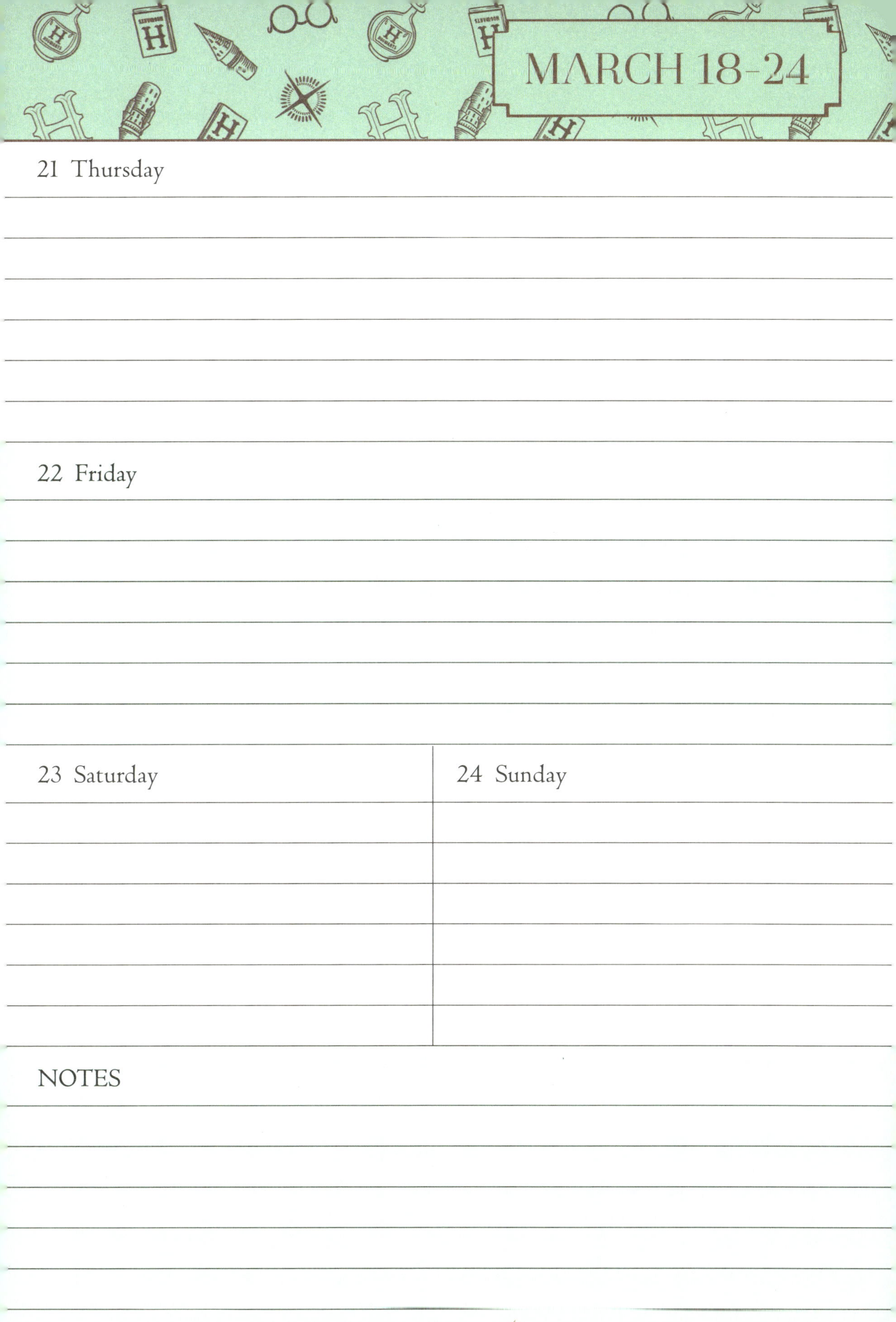

21 Thursday

22 Friday

23 Saturday

24 Sunday

NOTES

25 Monday

26 Tuesday

27 Wednesday

NOTES

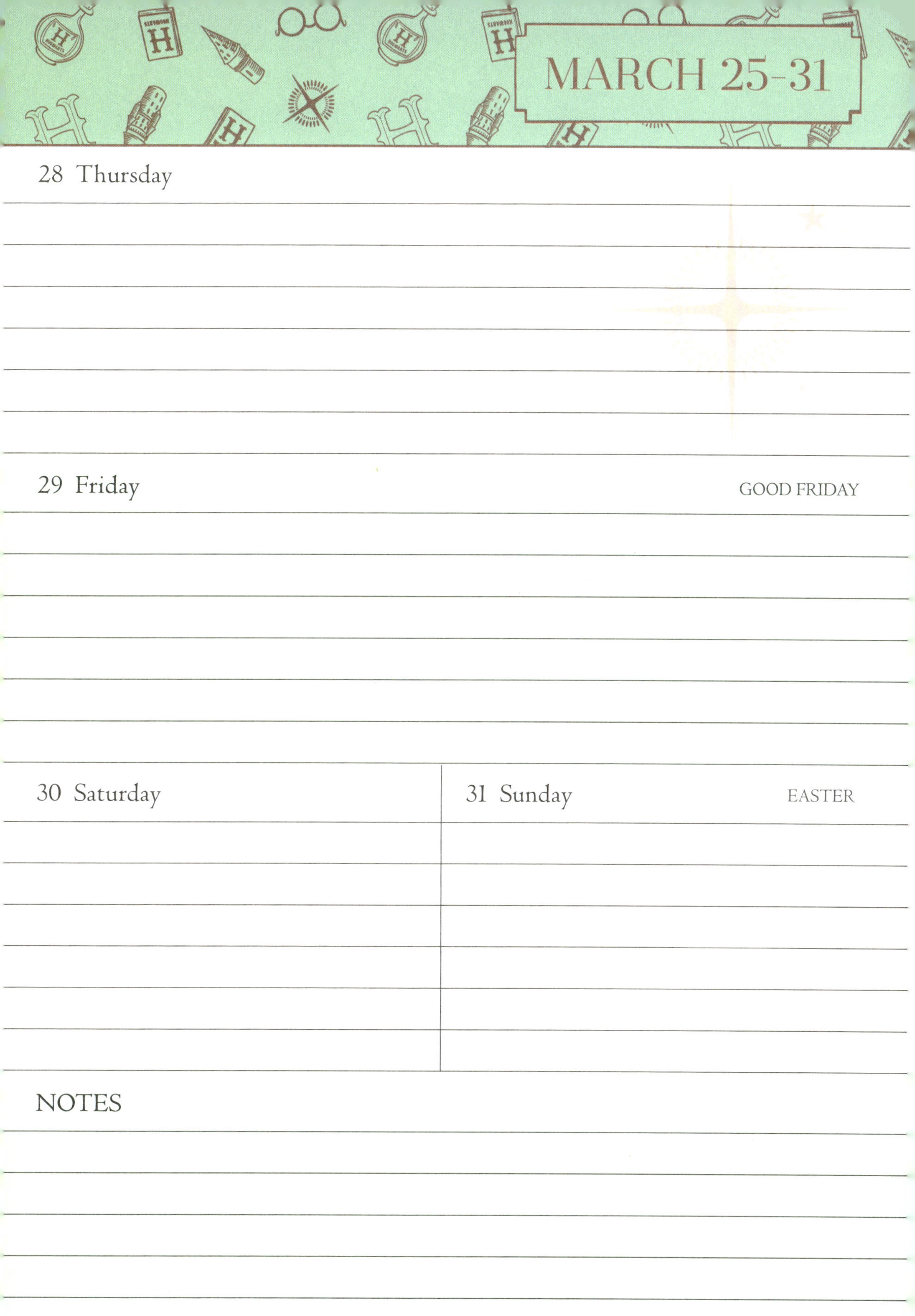

28 Thursday

29 Friday   GOOD FRIDAY

30 Saturday

31 Sunday   EASTER

NOTES

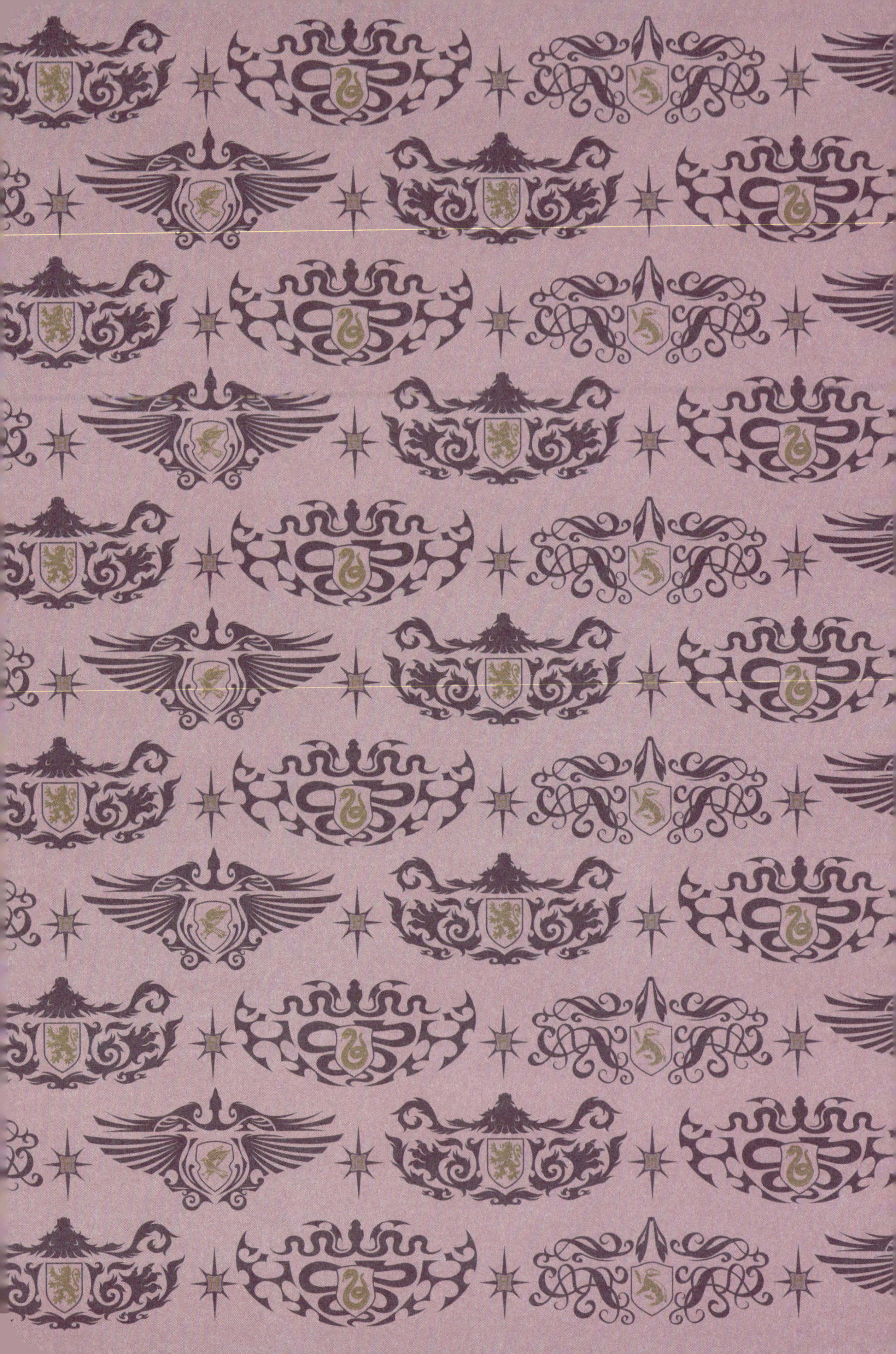

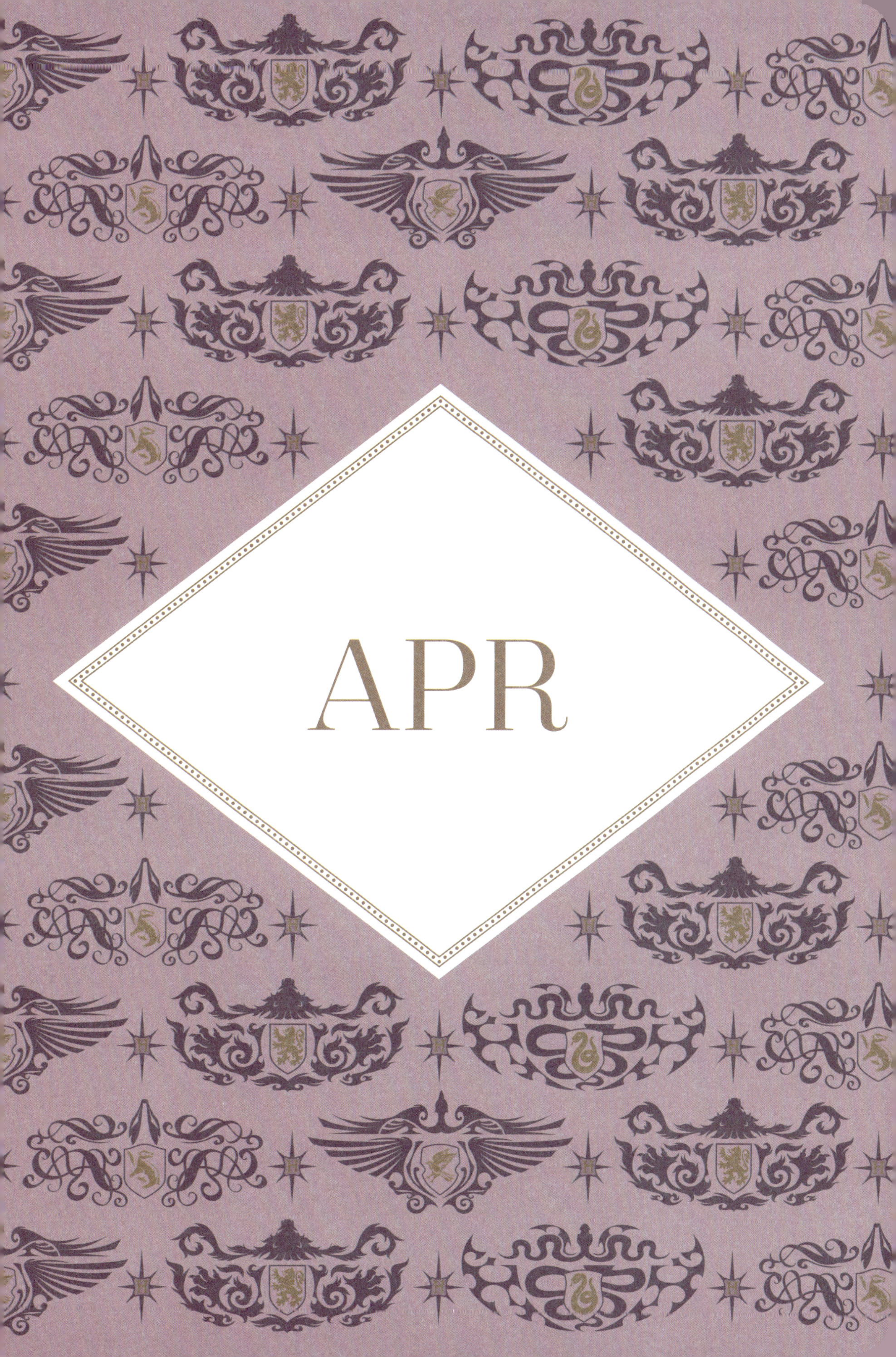
APR

APRIL 2024

SUNDAY	MONDAY	TUESDAY	WEDNESDAY
	1 April Fools' Day Easter Monday	2	3
7	8	9	10
14	15	16	17
21	22 First Day of Passover Earth Day	23	24
28	29	30	

THURSDAY	FRIDAY	SATURDAY	Notes
4	5	6	
11	12	13	
18	19	20	
25	26	27	

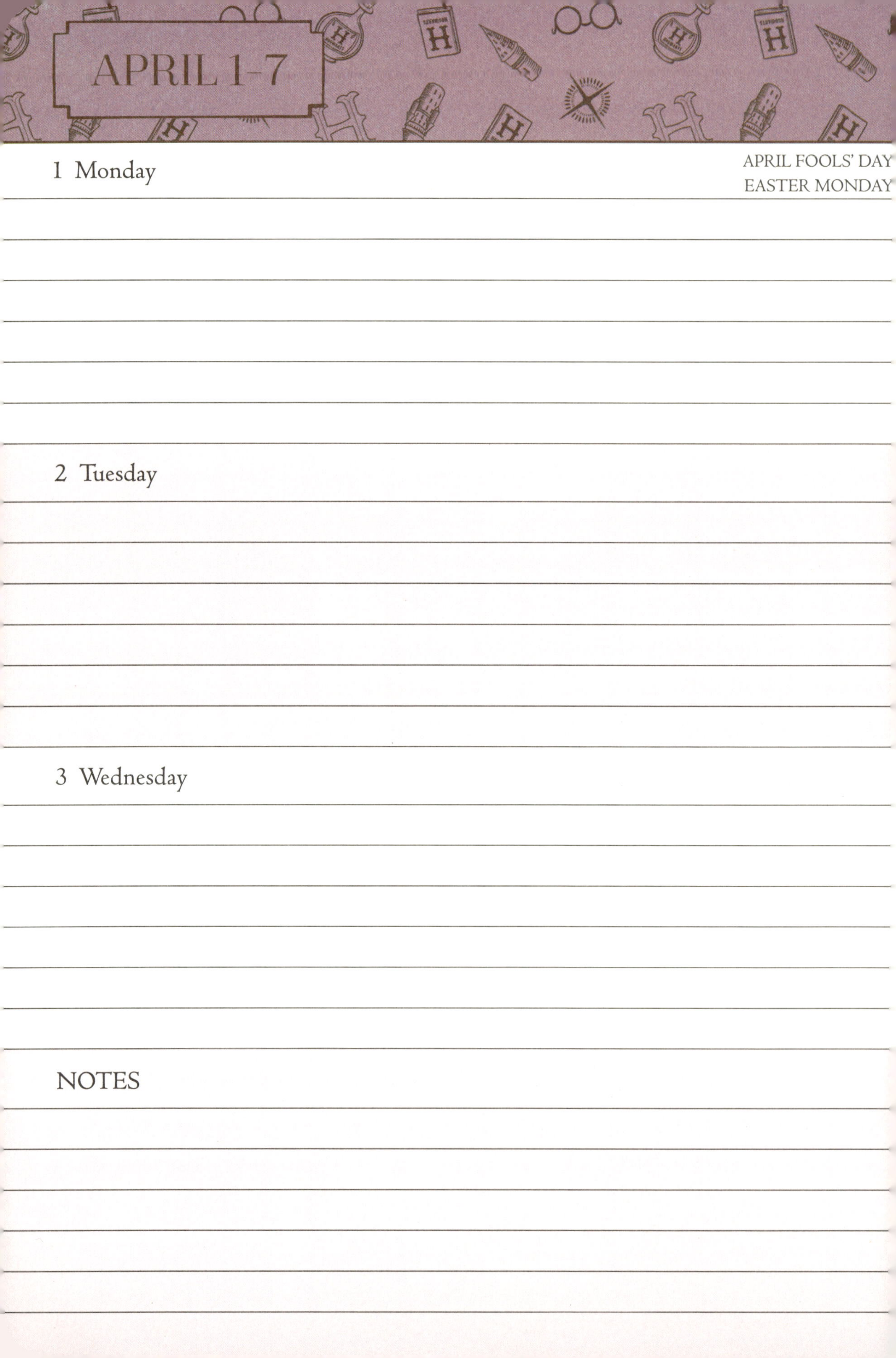

1 Monday

APRIL FOOLS' DAY
EASTER MONDAY

2 Tuesday

3 Wednesday

NOTES

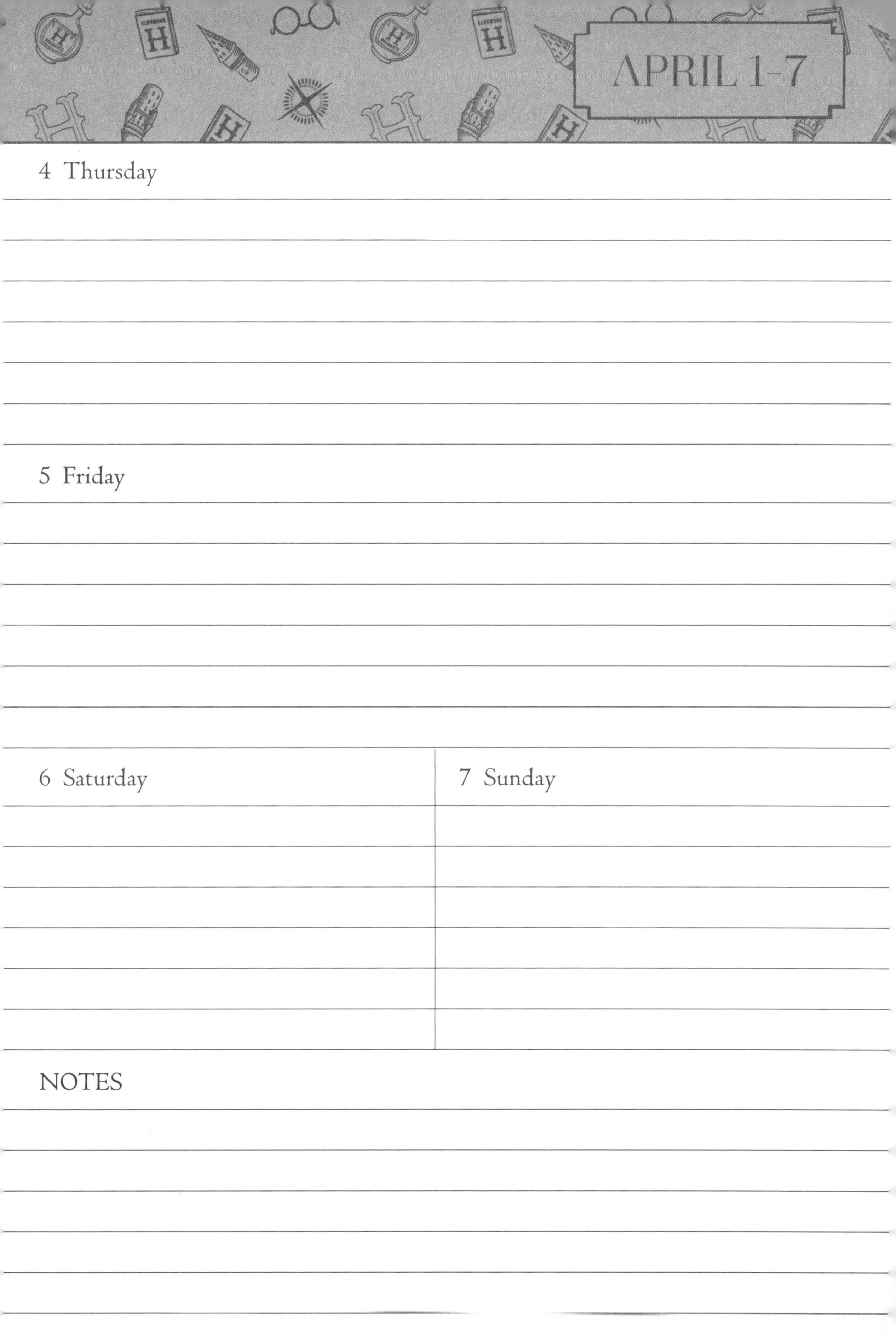

4 Thursday

5 Friday

6 Saturday

7 Sunday

NOTES

8 Monday

9 Tuesday

10 Wednesday

NOTES

11 Thursday

12 Friday

13 Saturday

14 Sunday

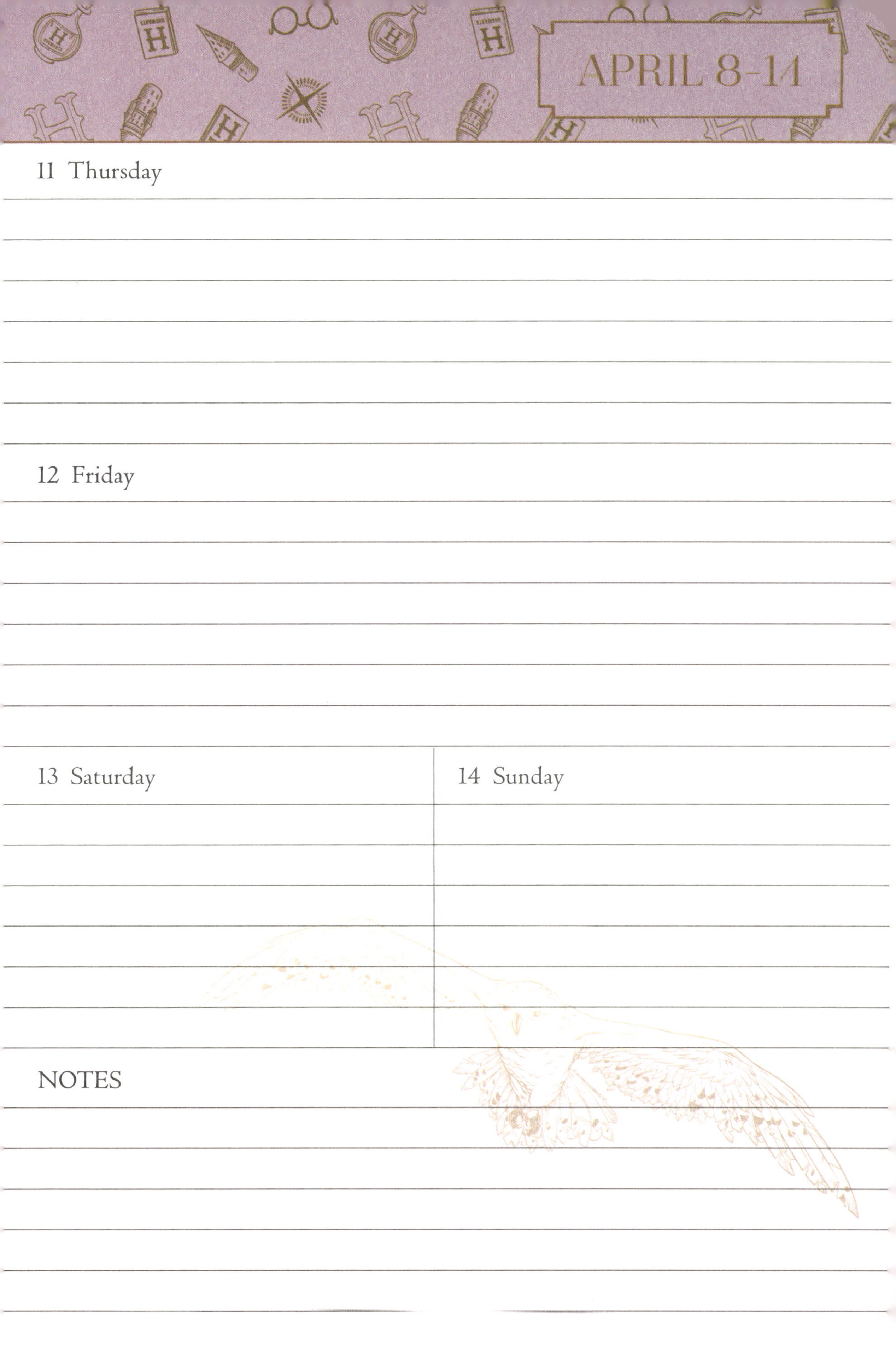

NOTES

15 Monday

16 Tuesday

17 Wednesday

NOTES

18 Thursday

19 Friday

20 Saturday

21 Sunday

NOTES

22 Monday

23 Tuesday

24 Wednesday

NOTES

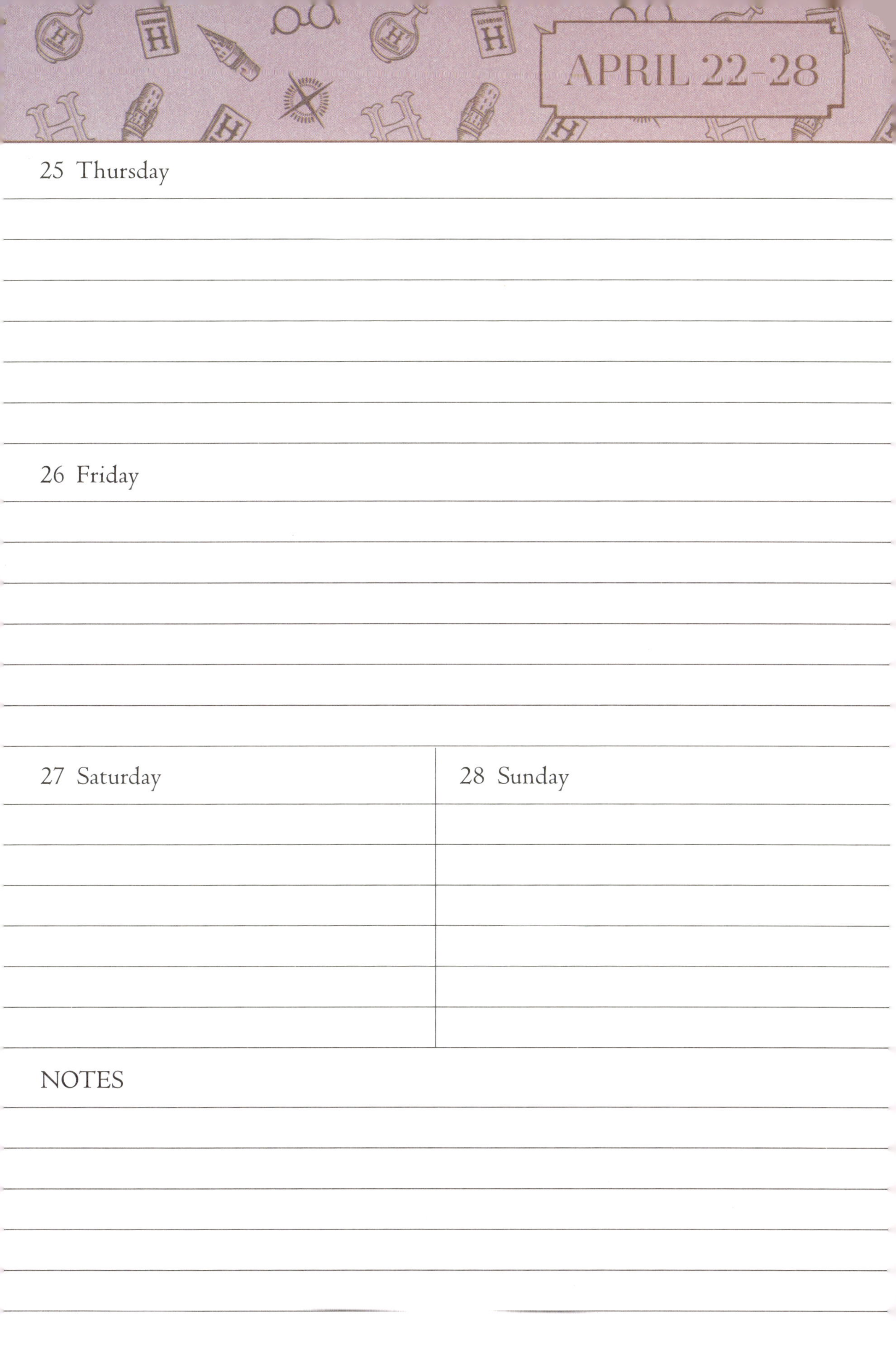

25 Thursday

26 Friday

27 Saturday

28 Sunday

NOTES

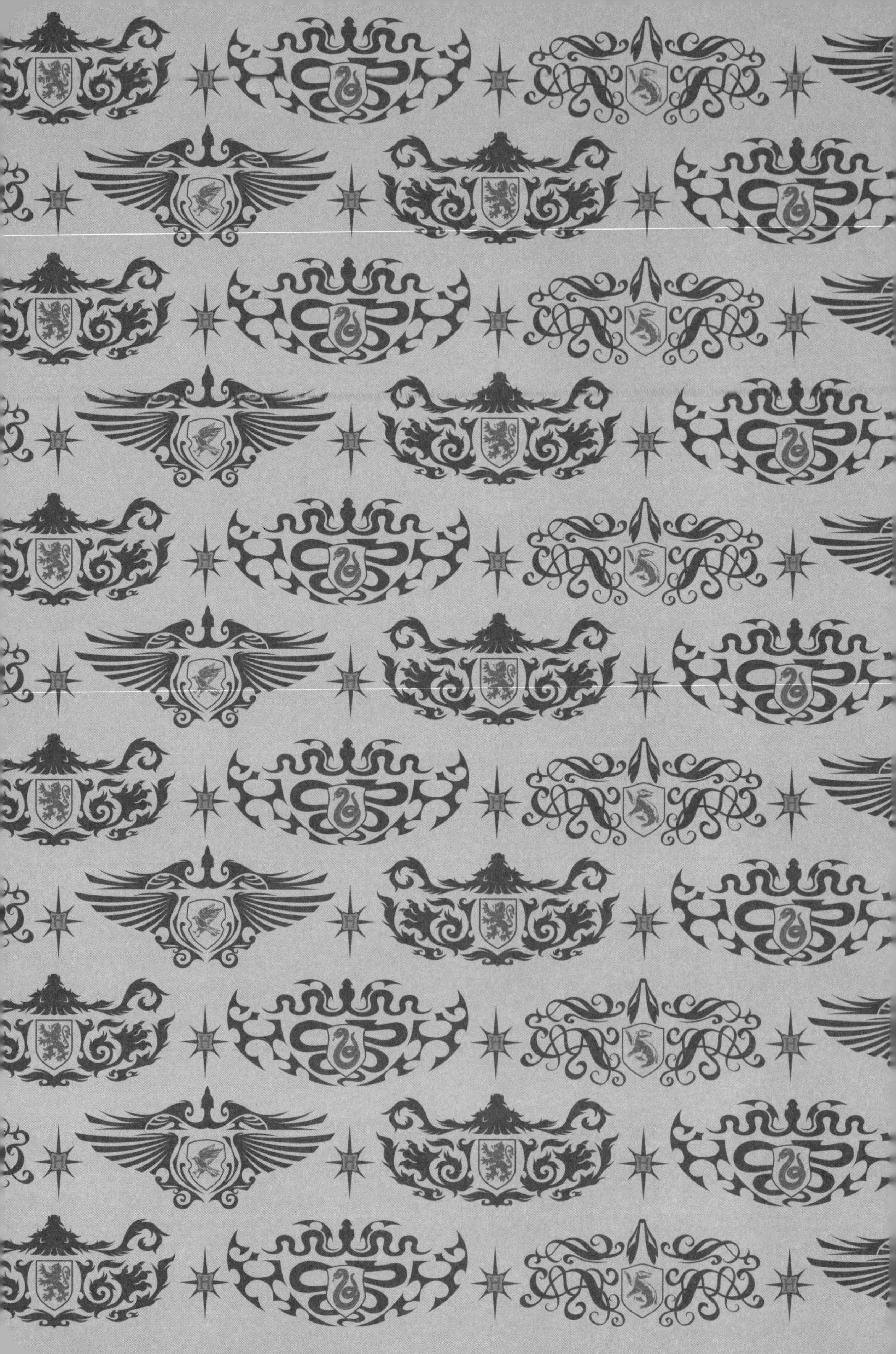

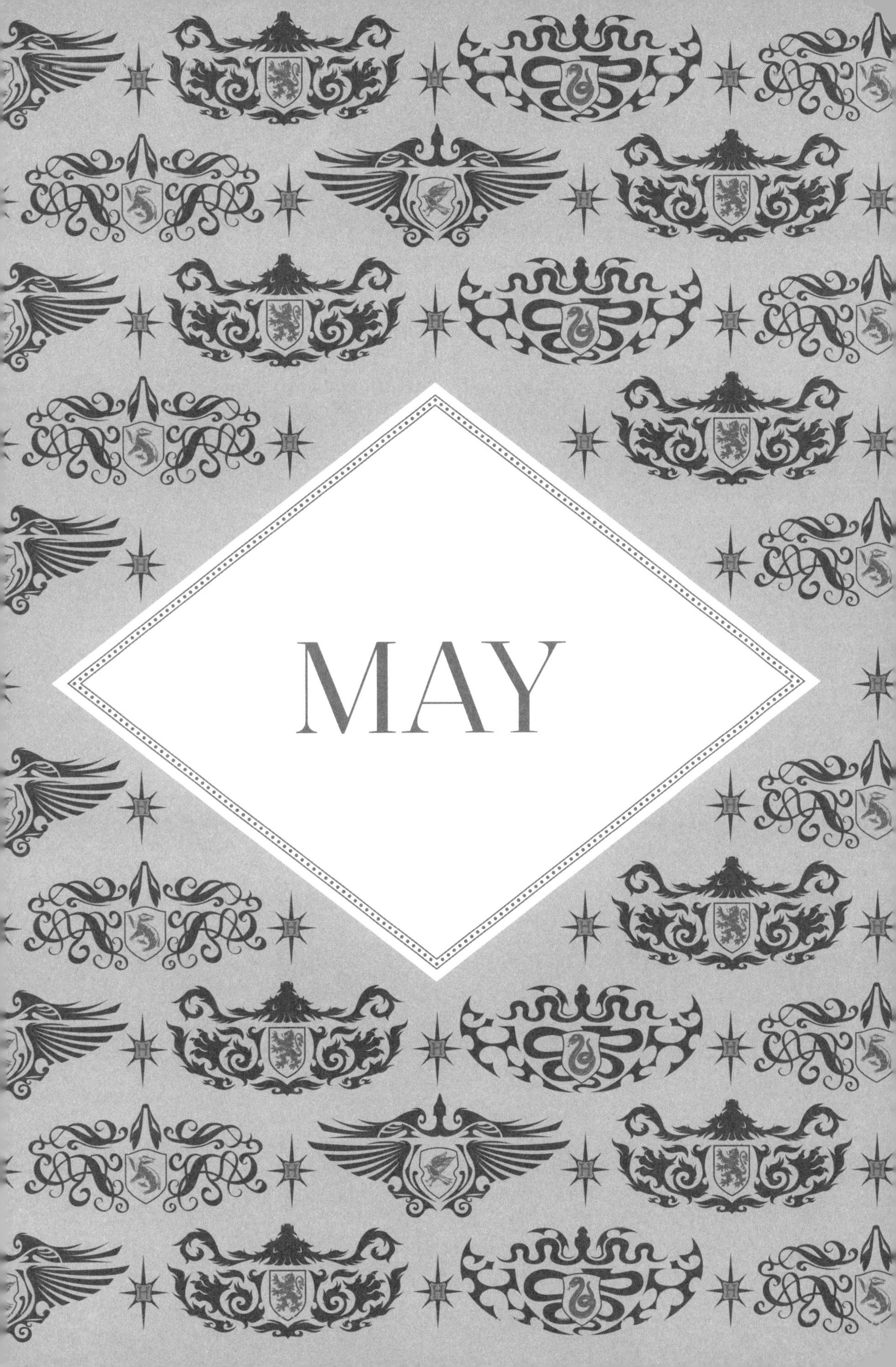
MAY

MAY 2024

SUNDAY	MONDAY	TUESDAY	WEDNESDAY
			1
5	6 Early May Bank Holiday (UK)	7	8
12 Mother's Day	13	14	15
19	20	21	22
26	27 Memorial Day Spring Bank Holiday (UK)	28	29

MAY 2024

THURSDAY	FRIDAY	SATURDAY	Notes
2 Anniversary of the Battle of Hogwarts	3	4	
9	10	11	
16	17	18	
23	24	25	
30	31		

29 Monday

30 Tuesday

1 Wednesday

NOTES

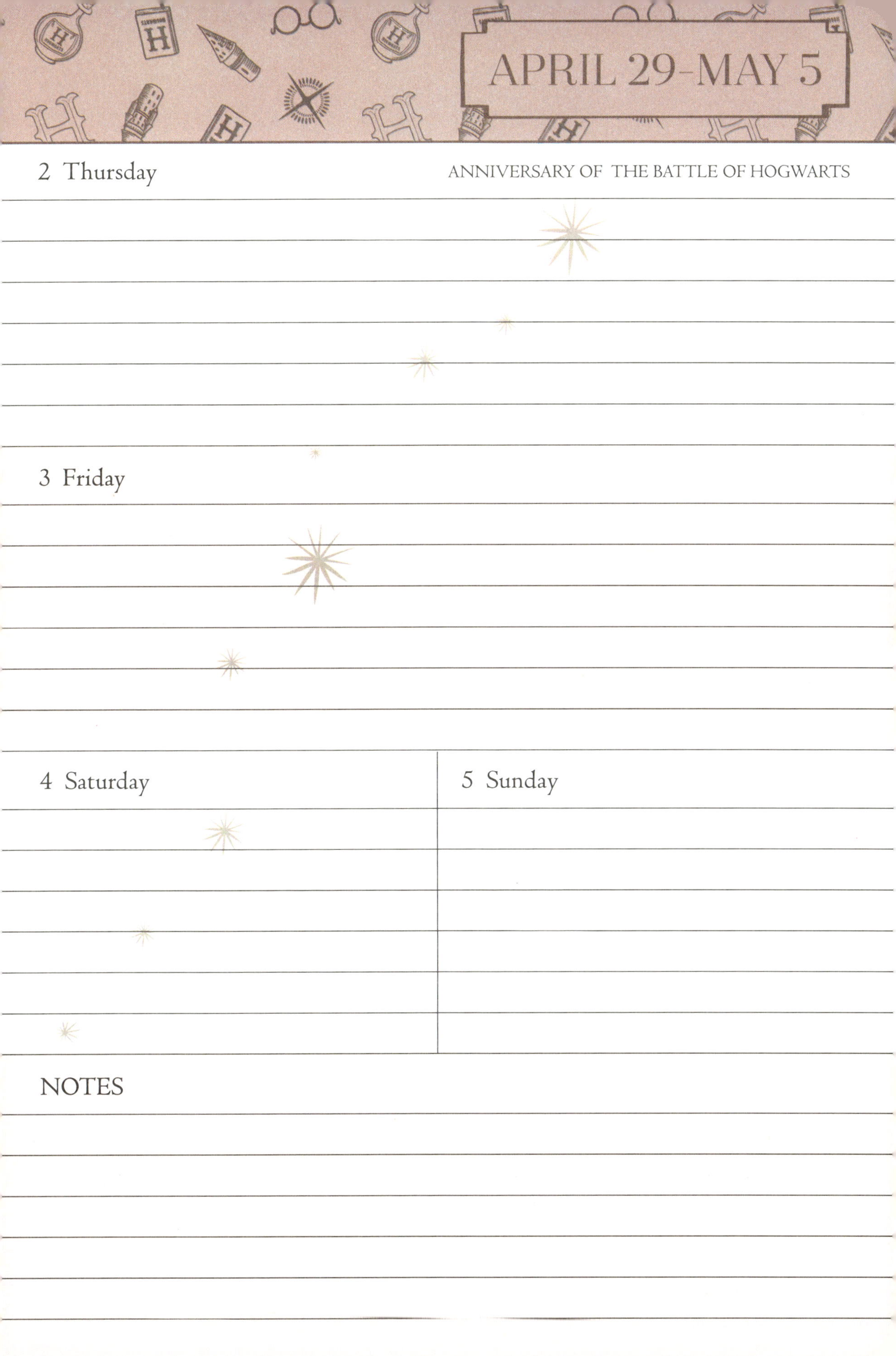

2 Thursday

ANNIVERSARY OF THE BATTLE OF HOGWARTS

3 Friday

4 Saturday

5 Sunday

NOTES

6 Monday

EARLY MAY BANK HOLIDAY (UK)

7 Tuesday

8 Wednesday

NOTES

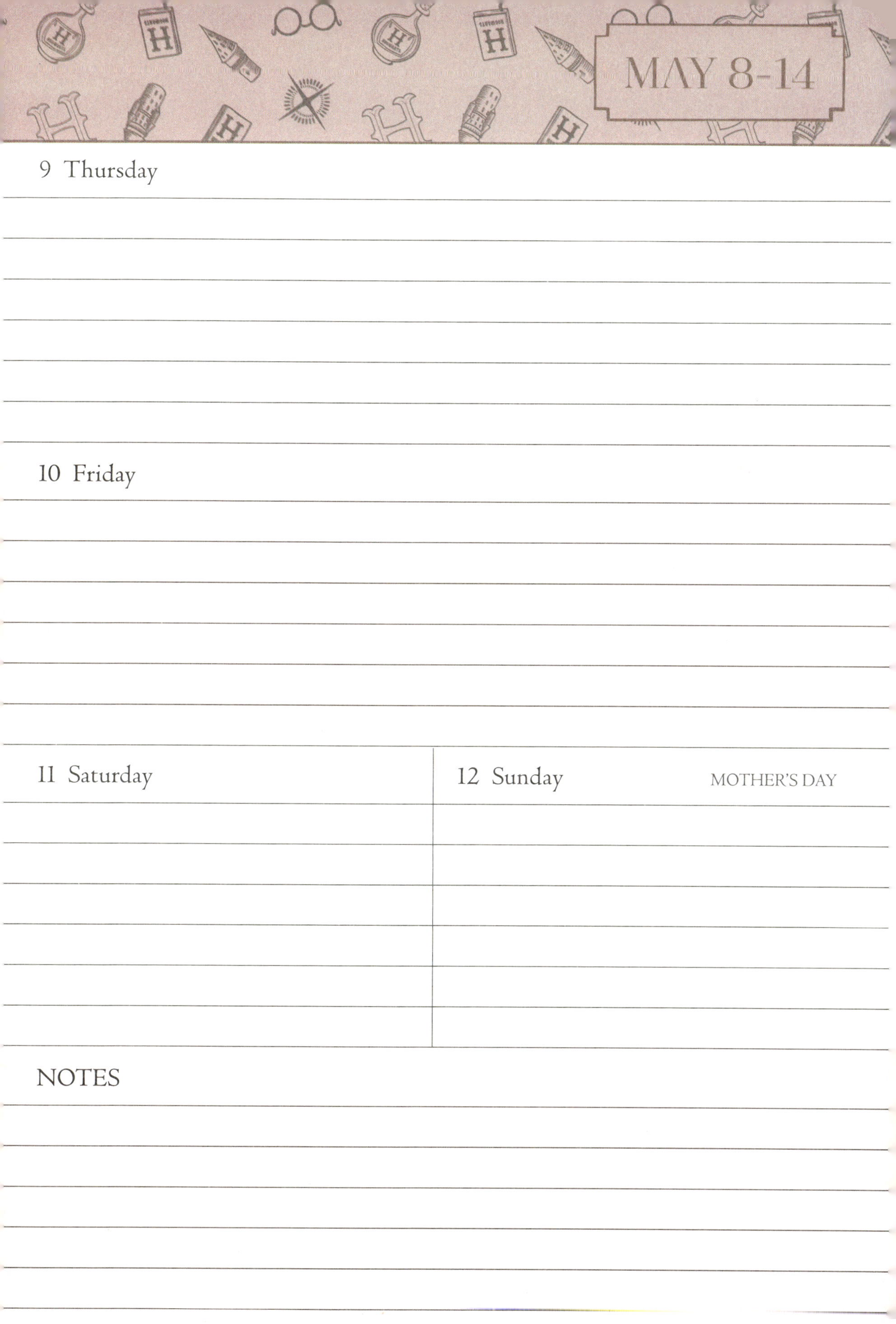

9 Thursday

10 Friday

11 Saturday

12 Sunday   MOTHER'S DAY

NOTES

13 Monday

14 Tuesday

15 Wednesday

NOTES

16 Thursday

17 Friday

18 Saturday

19 Sunday

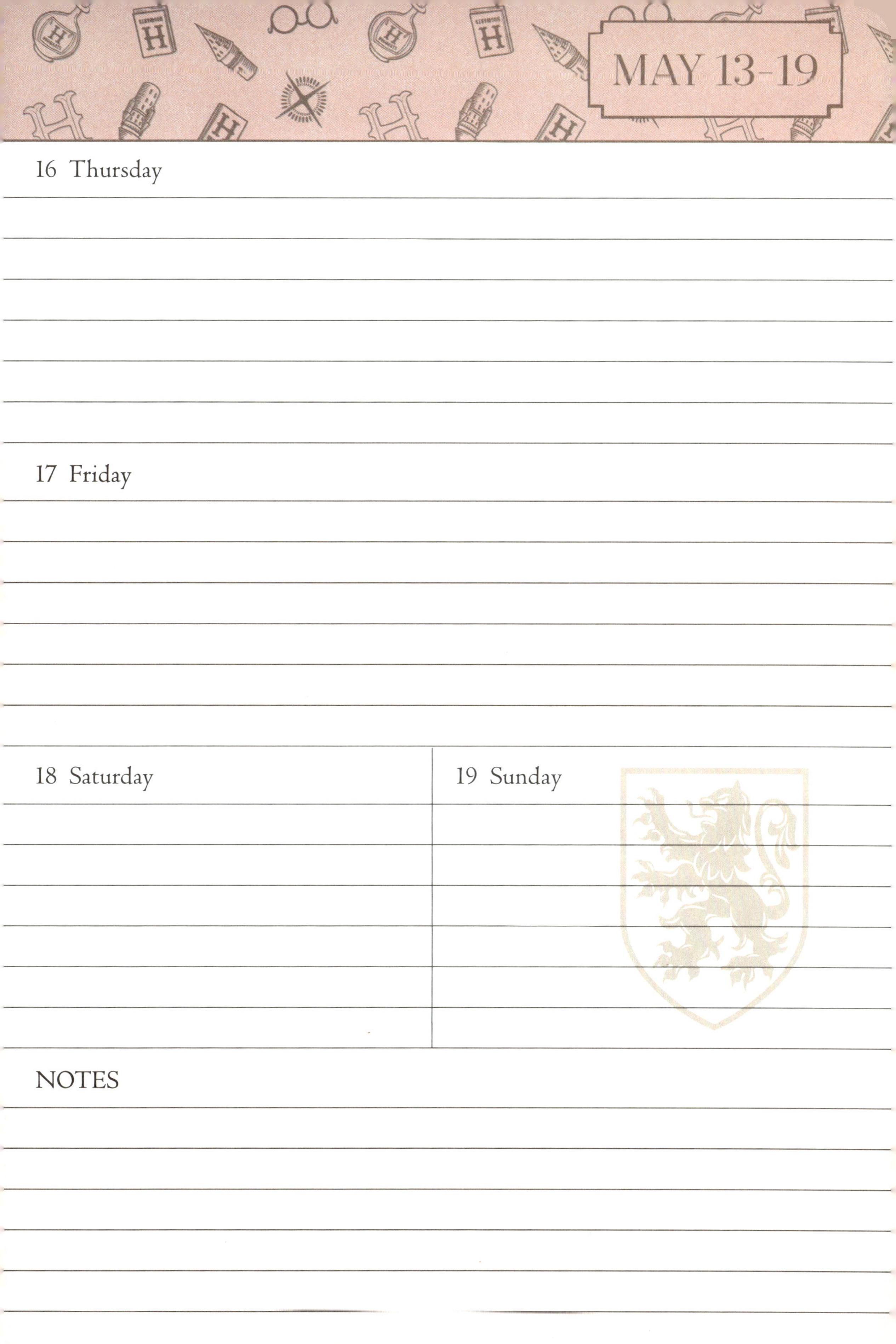

NOTES

20 Monday

21 Tuesday

22 Wednesday

NOTES

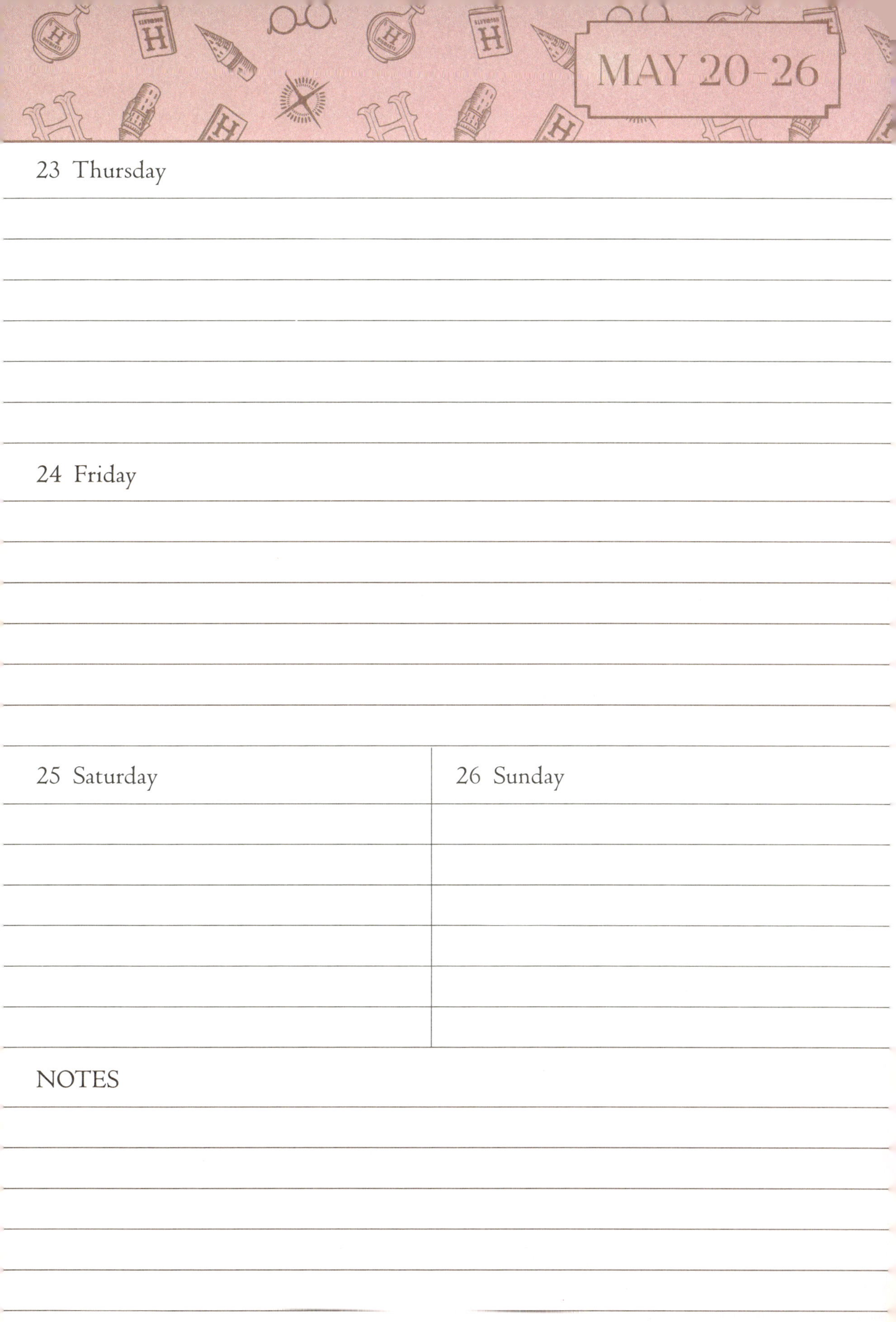

23 Thursday

24 Friday

25 Saturday

26 Sunday

NOTES

27 Monday

MEMORIAL DAY
SPRING BANK HOLIDAY (UK)

28 Tuesday

29 Wednesday

NOTES

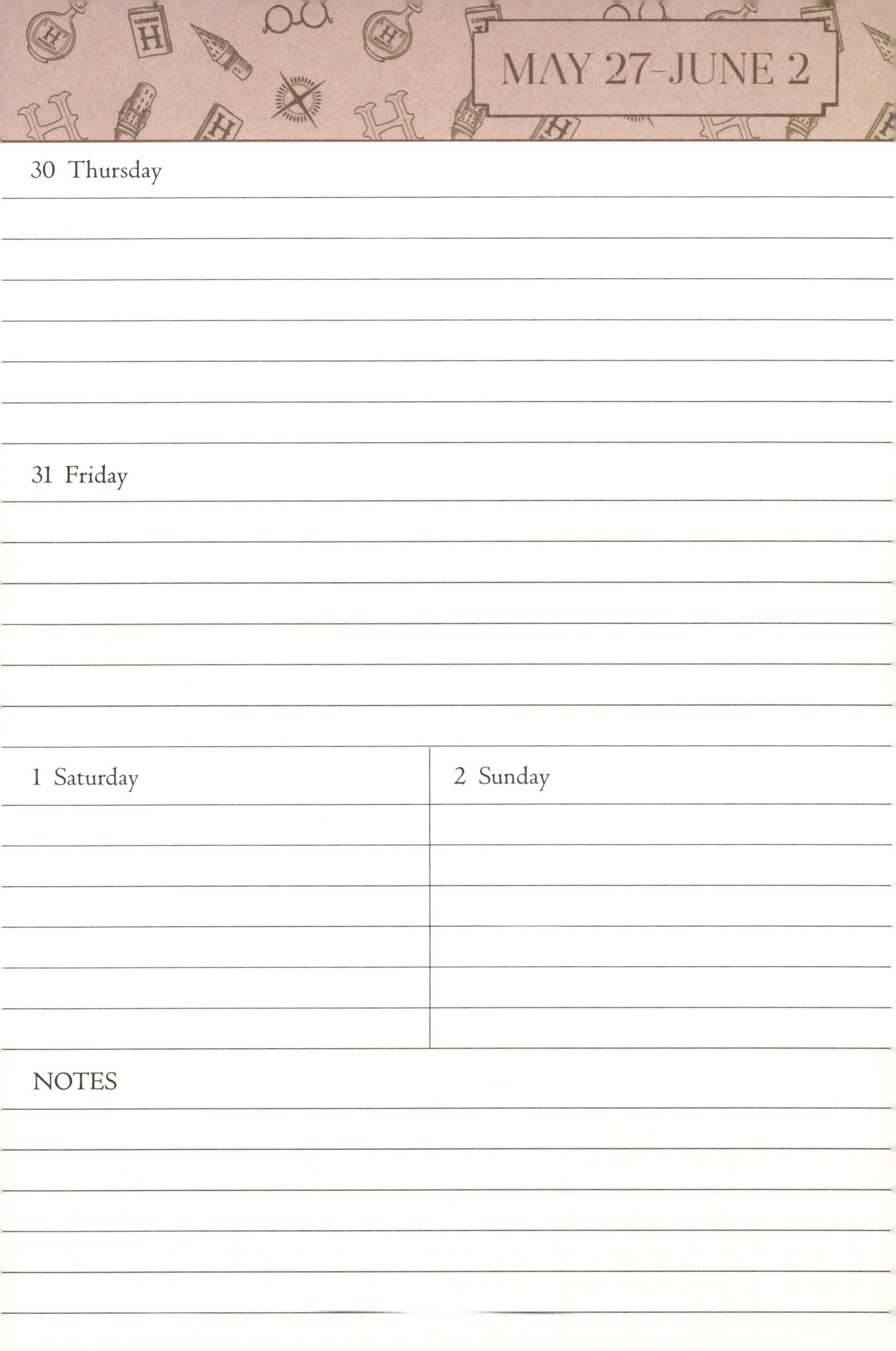

30 Thursday

31 Friday

1 Saturday

2 Sunday

NOTES

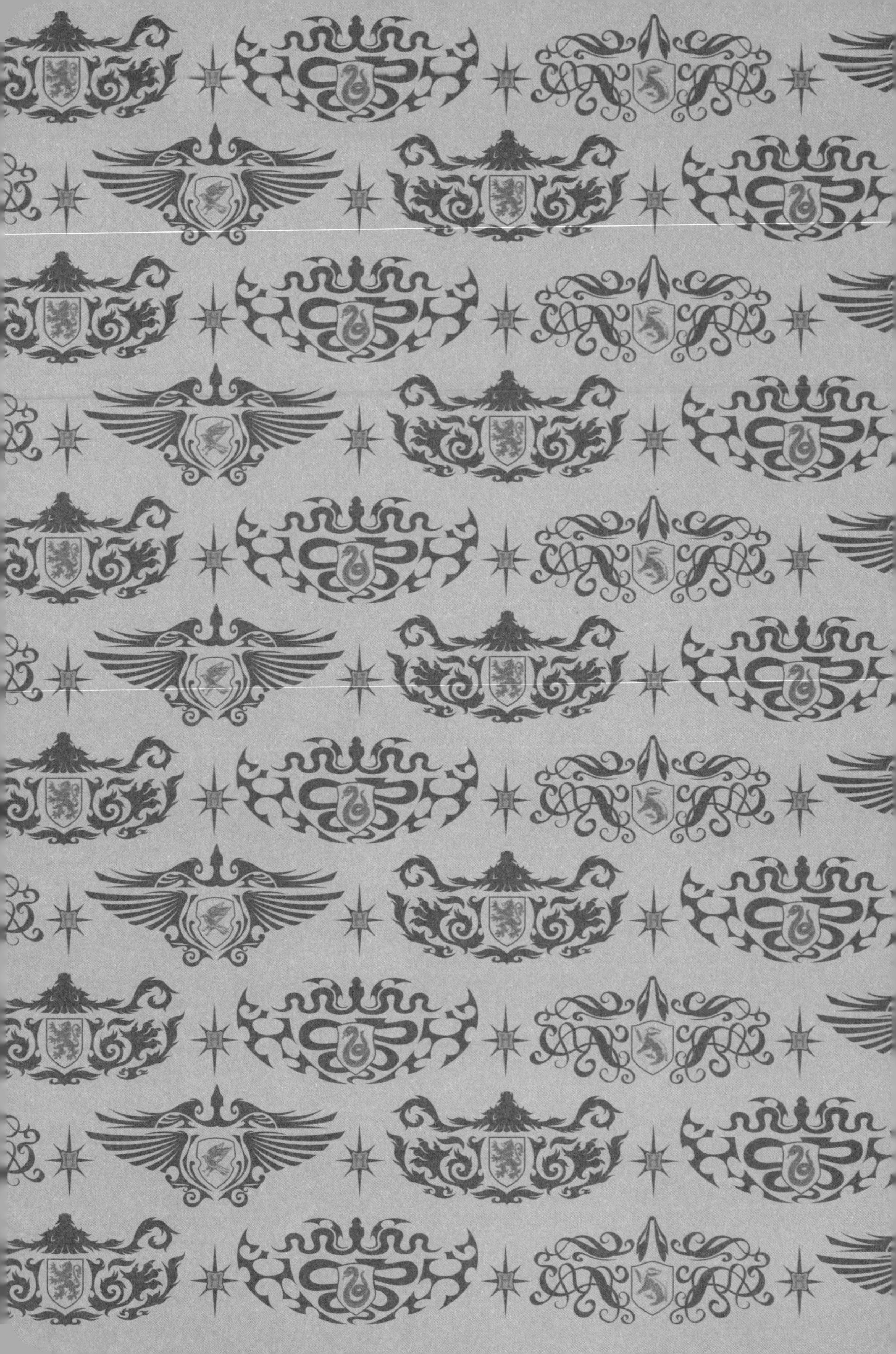

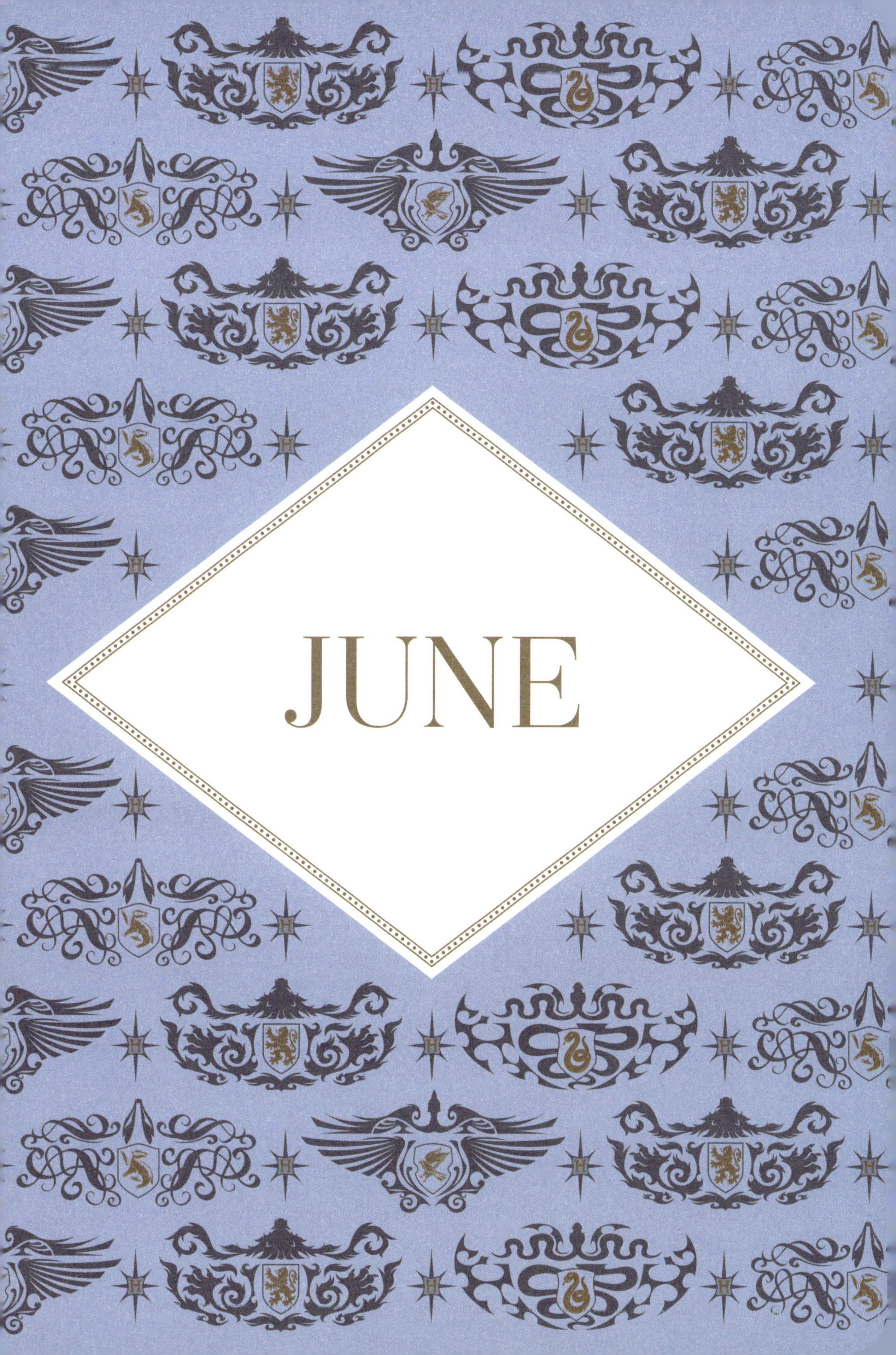
JUNE

SUNDAY	MONDAY	TUESDAY	WEDNESDAY
2	3	4	5
9	10	11	12
16	17	18	19
Father's Day			Juneteenth
23	24	25	26
30			

JUNE 2024

THURSDAY	FRIDAY	SATURDAY	Notes
		1	
6	7	8	
13	14	15	
20	21	22	
27	28	29	

3 Monday

4 Tuesday

5 Wednesday

NOTES

6 Thursday

7 Friday

8 Saturday

9 Sunday

NOTES

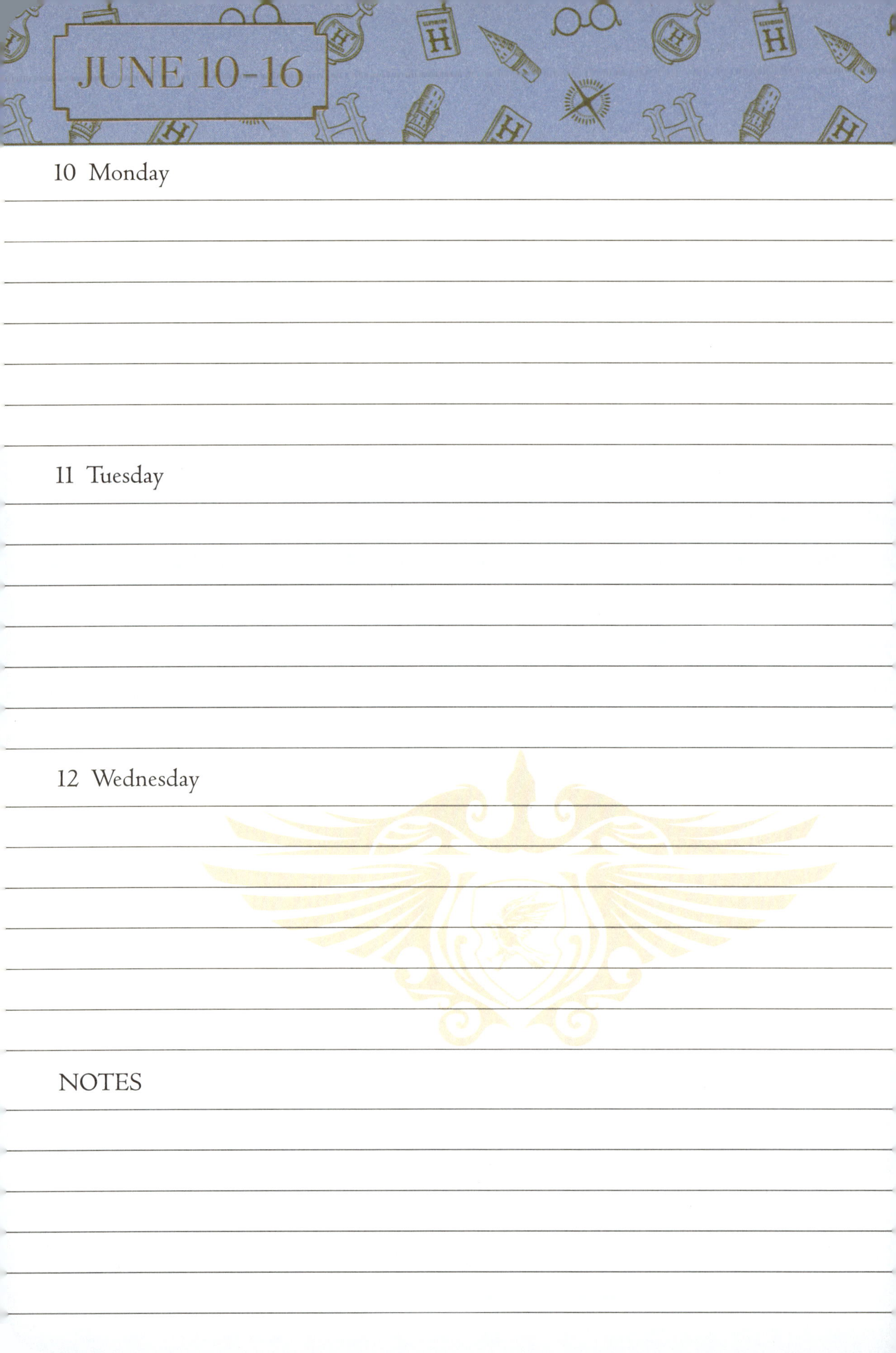

10 Monday

11 Tuesday

12 Wednesday

NOTES

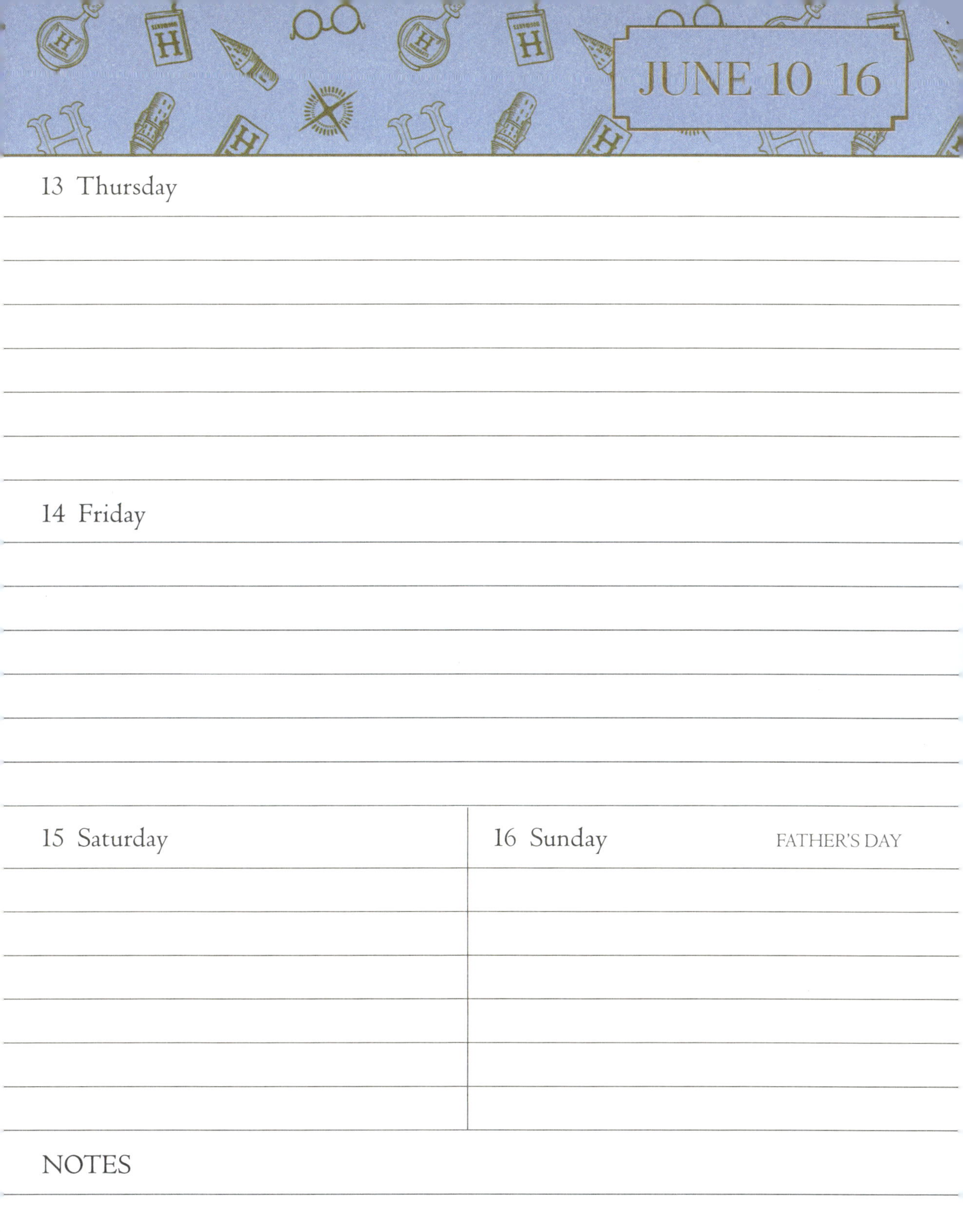

13 Thursday

14 Friday

15 Saturday

16 Sunday — FATHER'S DAY

NOTES

17 Monday

18 Tuesday

19 Wednesday   JUNETEENTH

NOTES

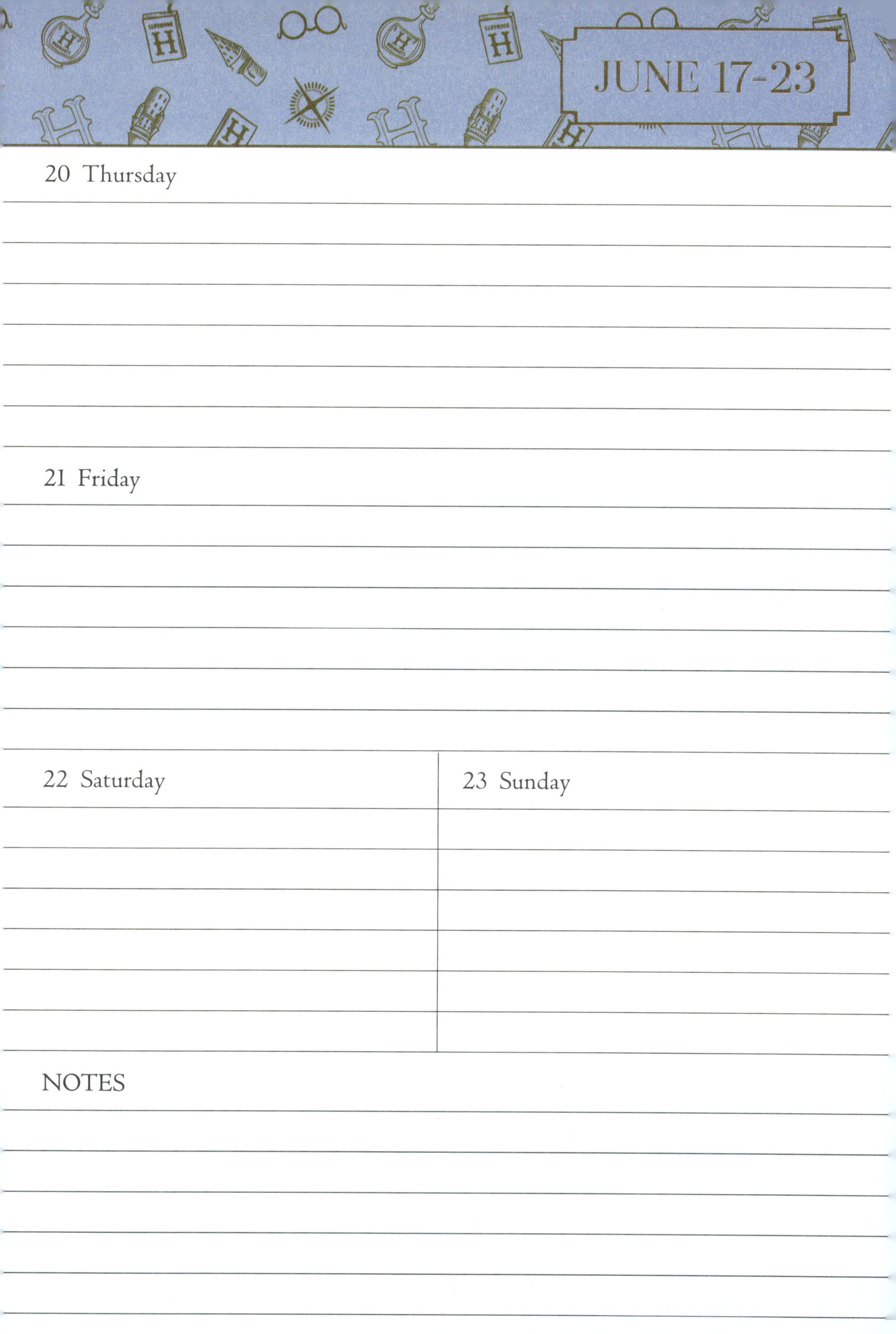

20 Thursday

21 Friday

22 Saturday

23 Sunday

NOTES

24 Monday

25 Tuesday

26 Wednesday

NOTES

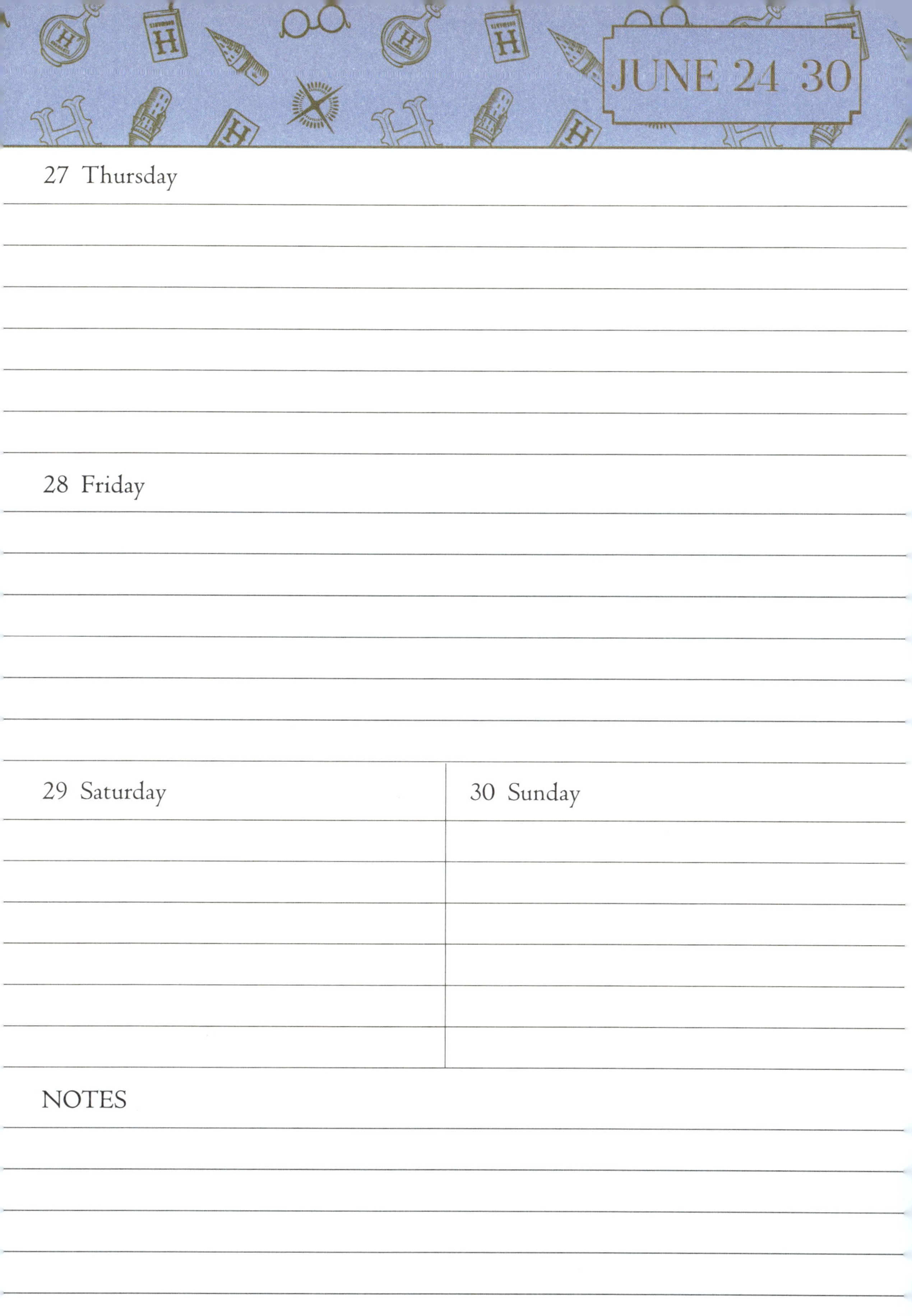

27 Thursday

28 Friday

29 Saturday

30 Sunday

NOTES

NOTES

NOTES

NOTES

NOTES

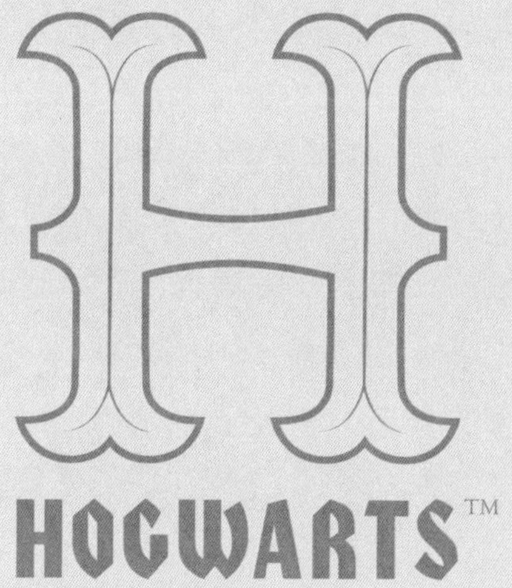